THE
WANTED
THE UNAUTHORIZED BIOGRAPHY

THE WANTED

THE UNAUTHORIZED BIOGRAPHY

CHAS NEWKEY-BURDEN

Michael O'Mara Books Limited

This paperback edition first published in 2013.

First published in hardback in Great Britain in 2010 by
Michael O'Mara Books Limited
9 Lion Yard
Tremadoc Road
London SW4 7NQ

A CIP catalogue record for this book is available from the British
Library.

Papers used by Michael O'Mara Books Limited are natural, recyclable
products made from wood grown in sustainable forests. The
manufacturing processes conform to the environmental regulations of
the country of origin.

ISBN: 978-1-78243-039-1 in paperback print format
ISBN: 978-1-84317-966-5 in ePub format
ISBN: 978-1-84317-967-2 in Mobipocket format

1 2 3 4 5 6 7 8 9 10

www.mombooks.com

Designed and typeset by K.DESIGN, Winscombe, Somerset
Plate section designed by Greg Stevenson

Printed in the UK by CPI Group (UK) Ltd, Croydon, CR0 4YY

CONTENTS

Prologue 7

1 Max George 15

2 Tom Parker 37

3 Siva Kaneswaran 55

4 Jay McGuiness 71

5 Nathan Sykes 85

6 The Max Factor 109

7 The Boy Band 143

8 Too Cool for Schools 161

9 All Time Highs 189

10 Into Tomorrow 209

11 The American Dream 223

Acknowledgements 245

Picture Credits 245

Index 247

PROLOGUE

It is the dream of every pop act to have a number one hit. The harsh reality is that most will never achieve that dream, however hard they try, or however wonderful their material. Even the lucky few that do enjoy a number one hit rarely reach that all-too-elusive target as quickly as The Wanted. But then, in the world of Max, Nathan, Tom, Jay and Siva, life is often exceptional…

Their first single, 'All Time Low', had all the makings of a chart-topping hit. The strings that begin the song are iconic and attention-grabbing. The song then builds wonderfully: the poetic, lyrical refrain about being 'in pieces', and how 'peace is' something that the protagonist will never know, was as deliciously infectious as pop music got in 2010. Towards the end of the recording, a song that had started with a sense of understated heartbreak and despondency explodes into a defiant, hands-in-the-air chant. It is a dance-floor filling moment that hints at better times to come for the song's heartbroken hero. The track then closes with a return to the gentler mood of its beginnings. The pop market had rarely known a song to so perfectly sum up the gamut of emotions people go through after a romantic break-up.

In the run-up to the single's release, Max had admitted he was genuinely hoping to get a number one hit with the song. All the same, he was realistic. He had tasted the bitterness of pop disappointment with a previous boy band, called Avenue. Max showed how nervous he was when he said of 'All Time Low's prospects, 'But, like, it's so hard, innit? Top five would be awesome.' It would be, but number one would be even better.

As for young Nathan, he had predicted 'All Time Low' would finish no higher than number forty-one. He was joking, but Nathan's comment demonstrated that the band were not taking anything for granted. But still, they dreamed.

It was a nervous week in The Wanted's shared south London home. The band felt on edge, and more than a few fingernails were chewed on. Then, on the Thursday, the website Amazon announced that it had already sold its entire stock of CDs. This was a good sign, as was the band's position in the overall mid-week chart. What mattered to them most, however, was where they were at the *end* of the week, when the actual chart positions are declared. That news, when it finally came, was exactly what they had dreamed of: The Wanted were number one. They had outsold their nearest rivals (Yolanda B Cool vs D Cup with the single 'We No Speak Americano') by over 10,000 copies to claim the top spot.

They received the news and almost exploded with joy as all the tension lifted in a wonderful, life-affirming moment. They had been officially together only a matter of months, yet here they were at the top of the charts, ruling the land of pop.

'When we got told it was number one, it was just like … what?!' said Max, looking back later. 'So we're literally just trying to come down at the moment, from somewhere up in the clouds, wherever our heads are.'

As for Tom, he was in bullish mood. 'I genuinely believe the boy band thing is back,' he declared. He also took the time to compose a brief message of thanks to the fans, which was posted on The Wanted's official website. It read: 'You wouldn't believe how much we adore all you lot, you've got us to #1 and we owe it all to you :) – Tom xxxxxxxxxxxxxxxx'. Then there was more jumping, whooping and embracing. They had done it!

The band members got into their gladdest of glad rags and headed out for a proper celebration at the exclusive Whisky Mist club in London's super-posh Mayfair district. Whisky Mist is a plush establishment, where A-list celebrities and even members of the royal family are often seen partying. Very fitting surroundings for *the* pop band of the moment. It was a raucous night: there were toasts, cheers and laughter as the festivities continued and the boys partied hard. 'We'll leather it at any party. I like to get stuck into the booze,' Tom said.

International pop diva Leona Lewis joined them for a while, adding extra glamour to the party and sparking tabloid speculation of a potential dalliance between her and Max. The band bought some champagne fireworks as the evening wore on, and the comically accident-prone Tom somehow burnt one of his nipples with one of the drinks. It was that kind of night. 'Messy,' said Jay, looking back later with a wince.

It was only as the excitement died down that the band members suddenly remembered a promise they had made. 'We said if we get a number one, we're all going to run down our street naked,' recalled Jay. That would have been a welcome spectacle. Every member of The Wanted is a heart-throb, and each has a distinctive look. There is Siva, who is tall, dark, smouldering and the owner of a pair of cheekbones many a supermodel – male or female – would die for. Jay is the other giant of the band, but his height is offset by his sweet face and curly, flopping hair. Then there is Tom, spiky of both hair and facial features – the boy-next-door that girls would love to peek over the fence at. Sweeter still is the youngest band member Nathan, the real boy of the boy band with cute features that have broken many a heart. Then there is the more imposing presence of their de facto leader, Max, the crop-haired, more muscular hunk of The Wanted.

At the time of writing, the band have yet to run down any street naked. If that day ever comes, they can count on an enormous and hysterical audience. You'd better be able to run fast, boys ...

▶▶▶1 MAX GEORGE

Full name: Maximillian
   Alberto George
Hometown: Manchester
Date of birth: 6 September 1988
Star sign: Virgo
Height: 5'8"
Eyes: grey
Hair: dark brown
Favourite food: Dominos pizza,
   full English breakfast,
   rare steak
Favourite band: Queen
Football team: Manchester City
Favourite animal: Great white
   shark
Favourite TV show: *The X Factor*

So let's start with the young man who is so often in the middle of the line-up. Quite fittingly, given his role as the big brother of the band, Max George has probably the most eventful life-story of all the members of The Wanted. Even before he joined the smash-hit boy band, Max had already tasted the highs and lows of the rollercoaster world of celebrity. At first he did not succeed, but Max tried and tried again. Having been sucked in by, and then spat out of, the entertainment industry, he has developed not just a thick skin, but also a finely tuned perspective on the ways of show business. As such, he can provide a shrewd soul for the other band members to turn to when they need a bit of advice. He has a wisdom in these matters far beyond his years.

It all started in the north-west of England. Maximillian Alberto George was born on 6 September 1988. On the very same day, 2,000 items of Elton John's personal memorabilia – including some outrageous feather boas – were auctioned at Sotheby's in London, and the smooth tones of Phil Collins's song 'A Groovy Kind Of Love' were filling the airwaves of Britain. While Collins occupied the number one slot in the singles chart, the album chart was topped by another legendary solo singer – Kylie Minogue. The solo-star-dominated chart on the day of his birth seems fitting, as Max has sometimes been spoken of as a future solo star by those who have observed his central role in The Wanted. He is certainly the member who shows most initial signs of the charisma required for such a role. But long before he even became involved in music he had another big passion – football. It was while he was a schoolboy that he first fell for the charms of the beautiful game.

Max attended Bolton School, which was founded hundreds of years ago, in the sixteenth century. It has since become one of the north of England's most respected independent schools. It is one of the biggest, too, with well over 2,000 pupils currently on its books. Many of those who have attended the celebrated independent school down the years have then gone on to become famous themselves. Among these are leading British actor Sir Ian McKellen and also *Royle Family* star Ralf Little, as well as best-selling author Monica Lee. Max is but the latest graduate of Bolton School to find fame in the arts world. He loved going to school and then rushing home to watch his favourite kids' TV show: *Teenage Mutant Ninja Turtles*. 'They were awesome,' he remembered. As we will see, he is a fan of lizards, too.

The school's motto is the Latin phrase: *Mutare Vel Timere Sperno*, which means 'I spurn to change or to fear'. Max has rarely seemed to be someone who fears anything. He is a brave, almost soldier-like young man. His rise from his north-west England childhood to pop stardom is an inspiring tale, brimful of courage and determination. Make no mistake; there have been more than a few obstacles thrown in his way. He has experienced setbacks as well as the successes. Although there have been moments of disillusionment and despair, Max has always striven to look on the bright side and to bounce back from disappointment. For this positive, determined attitude he is being rewarded handsomely with his success and fame with The Wanted. Few could begrudge him the kind hand that fate has ultimately dealt him – he deserves it for staying true to himself and never giving up on his dreams.

However, some would say that Max's destiny was written in the stars from the start. The Virgo star sign he was born under is one dominated by creativity and efficiency, according to those who believe in astrology. Virgos are also widely believed to be perfectionists with a calm determination. The fact that Virgo is an artistic sign is best demonstrated by the fact that one of the most famous Virgos from history is perhaps the most celebrated pop star of all time, the late, great Michael Jackson. As a kid, Max enjoyed Jackson's music and studied his moves.

One aspect of Max that does not fit quite so neatly with the star sign is his love of lizards. He has owned many lizards as pets over the years, once having six of the little creatures at a time. He had, he told *Metro*, one favourite. 'She's called Adrienne. I named her after [fictional boxing star played by Sylvester Stallone] Rocky's wife. She's dead tame and is happy to come out of the tank. She eats like a pig.' Lizards are increasingly popular among celebrities: other pop stars to own such pets include Dougie Poynter, the rather phwoarsome bassist of McFly. As we shall see, another member of The Wanted also keeps them as pets.

For Max, though, his first love as a kid was football rather than music. He grew up as a fan of Manchester City but Max isn't satisfied with just watching football – he also loves playing the sport. Like many lads from the north-west of England, Max has kicked a ball about for as long as he can remember. Unlike many of those lads, though, Max quickly showed he had a genuine flair for the game. He is a committed fan of Manchester City, a side that have for so

twittertwittertwittertwittertwittertwittertwittertwittertwittertwittertwittertwitter

MaxTheWanted I actually adore every single fan we have!! X

6:32 PM Jul 26th via ÜberTwitter

long lived under the shadow of their legendary neighbours Manchester United. However, that comparative lack of success has formed a special bond between those who follow Manchester's second club. City fans like Max have learned to make the most of any victories over United as, for some time, these have been few and far between. Much to Max's delight, though, thanks to considerable foreign investment, City are now a much more formidable proposition and have ambitions to knock United off the perch they have rested on for so long. Whether they manage to or not remains to be seen, but for fans like Max these are very exciting times in the world of football as they begin to believe that their team might outshine the mighty United.

As a child, Max dreamed of pulling on the light-blue shirt of Manchester City not as a fan, but as a first-team player. For a short while, it seemed this dream might come true. As a player, Max has represented his schools and districts and was soon noticed by a scout for the Radcliffe Borough team. The Radcliffe Borough Football Club was founded in the 1940s and its historical highlight to date came in 2000, a few years before Max joined the club. That was the season in which Radcliffe Borough reached the first round of the prestigious FA Cup. Although they lost to York City, to have appeared in such a high-profile match in 'the cup that cheers' in front of a record crowd of 2,495 was naturally the source of much excitement and joy for the fans.

By 2005 Max was a regular star in the club's youth team. He was a promising performer on the field, and a popular figure among his team-mates. Had things progressed differently for him, it is quite likely that Max could have built a successful career as a footballer, rather than a singer. If so, he would definitely have been a football pin-up to rival the likes of David Beckham, Frank Lampard and Cesc Fabregas.

However, a serious injury put paid to Max's hopes of making a career out of football. He was under the eye of Preston North End FC at the time, and claims that he was on the brink of signing a two-year professional deal with them when disaster struck. He had even played for England Schoolboys, something that many of the current full England team have done in their early careers.

It is a moment in his life he is naturally a bit sad to recall. 'Yeah, I snapped my hip flexor – the muscle that joins your groin to your hip,' he remembered of the injury that struck him at the age of sixteen. 'That pretty much ended my football career.' It was a moment that was painful physically, and then when the seriousness of the injury struck him, Max also had to overcome the mental pain of crushing disappointment. His first dream for an exciting and lucrative career lay in tatters. Quite a blow for a teenage boy to come to terms with, particularly a football-mad one like Max. To be fair, by his own admission Max has poor eyesight, so perhaps football at the highest level would have been a step too far for him even without this injury occurring, though that would have been of little comfort to him at the time.

Even now that a career in football seems out of the question for him, he continues to be a passionate supporter of Manchester City. Other famous fans of the light-blue side are former Oasis stars Liam and Noel Gallagher, cricketer Andrew

Flintoff and comedian Alan Carr. Max still loves football and whenever his busy pop schedule allows, he likes nothing more than a Friday night down the pub with his father and grandfather. As they sit and drink they talk about football – particularly their beloved Manchester City, the club being in the centre of some exciting times of late. He loves watching a match either live in the stadium or in front of a big screen in the pub. At such times Max is fond of singing the club's anthems, such as 'Blue Moon'. His is one of the more melodious voices at such moments – quite a contrast to the boisterous bellows of many footie fans! Max said during his time with his first band, Avenue, that no matter how famous he became in the future, he would always want to be able to visit the pub like any normal young man. 'If [huge fame] did happen, I'd just try and do everything normally,' he told *OK!* magazine. 'I'd still want to go down the pub. I don't think it would get that bad.'

twittertwittertwittertwittertwittertwittertwittertwittertwittertwittertwittertwitter

MaxTheWanted Just been to the gym … OUCH!!!

7:12 AM August 23rd via ÜberTwitter

"Once my footie career was over, singing was my dream."

Back in 2005, with his dreams of a career in football in shreds, Max could have been devastated. Many young men who have suffered such a crushing disappointment have reacted by giving up all dreams of an exciting life, and have withdrawn to more humdrum ambitions. Perhaps they were silly, they tell themselves, to have ever believed there was more to life than a nine-to-five job. But Max is not like most people. Although he took a job in a clothes shop, he was quickly removed from that. 'I got sacked ... after two weeks,' he said. 'The boss rang me at about midnight and I was out on the lash. The next day when I rang in sick they told me I was sacked.' But he need not have worried, as he had bigger plans which would in time come true. It was time for his second stab at a special, fame-bringing career. 'Once my

28

footie career was over, singing was my dream,' he said. 'I obviously grew up with Take That mania being from Manchester.'

First, though, he had to work hard to realize his new dream. So it was that in 2005 Max decided to try to make it in a different, but no less exciting, career path – as a pop star. His new ambition began with an audition on a well-known television show, ensuring that his journey would be made in the public eye from the very start. *The X Factor* is Britain's best-loved reality talent show. It was conceived, created and launched by infamous reality television judge Simon Cowell. The first series ran in 2004, and it has since become the dominant television show in the talent genre.

Simon Cowell had first found fame as a judge on the reality show *Pop Idol*. However, with *The X Factor* he actually owns and runs the show. It is his baby, though he has now developed it into a money-making beast that has topped the ratings charts and launched acts as successful as Leona Lewis, JLS and Alexandra Burke. True, there have been some flops as well – most notably the unlucky 'winners' Steve Brookstein and Leon Jackson. Overall, though, it is a show that many aspiring pop stars dream of winning, as the benefits can be huge.

Max entered the second series of *The X Factor*. He had seen Steve Brookstein win the first series and then flop in the wake of it. Indeed, Brookstein quickly fell out with and parted company from Simon Cowell and his record label. He became a bitter critic of the show, and his example serves as a warning to all of how things can go badly wrong, even for a winner. However, his poor fortune was not enough to put off many thousands of people from applying for a crack at the show themselves. Indeed, a total of 75,000 hopefuls auditioned overall in 2005. Max was one of those who lined up, wondering what the future might hold. The opening auditions came at a busy time for him, but he is a resourceful and plucky young man – so he made it work. The chance to audition in front of Simon Cowell is worth re-arranging a few things for, after all!

He was one of 45,000 people to audition in the 16–24 age category. The auditioning process is considerably more complicated than the televised show suggests. Max had to audition in front of the show's producers twice before he was able to face the judges on camera. He duly impressed the producers and was ushered through to perform in a proper audition. These can be nerve-racking experiences, but Max did his utmost to take the pressure in his stride. The most terrifying part can be facing the notoriously straight-talking Simon Cowell. In front of the real judges, Simon Cowell, Louis Walsh and Sharon Osbourne, all Max could do was to try his best and hope it was enough to impress them. Luckily, the key judge, Cowell, was very impressed with Max once he heard him sing. He even told him that he reminded him of the pop superstar Robbie Williams – a rare compliment!

Max has always admired Robbie's music and style, but his musical tastes are actually quite old-fashioned. 'I like older stuff,' he told *Metro*. 'I love Elvis, Stevie Wonder and Otis Redding. The newer artists I like are Michael Jackson and Oasis.' Indeed, he has said that the song he wishes he had written is 'Dock Of The Bay' by Otis Redding. 'I think he's one of the greatest soul singers of all time … that song is spot on'. All the same, he listened to and took on board the advice and reactions that Cowell and Walsh gave him from the start, including their observation that he is reminiscent of Robbie. 'They told me: "Just keep working at it and keep listening to the stuff you're into, you'll learn a lot from pros."' It was a great relief for Max that he had received such a positive reaction. Many other contestants were not so fortunate that year. For instance, Louis Walsh told one, 'You should stick with your job stacking shelves in Sainsbury's.' Cowell was, as usual, even more blunt. He told one hopeful: 'You've got to be kidding. That was loathsome – one of the corniest, worst auditions I've ever seen in my life.' Painful comments, which Max was definitely delighted to avoid.

These were very busy times for Max, as his father Mark explained. 'Max went to the first audition for a bit of

twittertwittertwittertwittertwittertwittertwittertwittertwittertwittertwittertwitter

MaxTheWanted On way back to London … with ELVIS!! (My dog.)

10:51 PM Aug 8th via ÜberTwitter

fun really, but he was really pleased to get as far as he did,' he said proudly. 'He sat and passed his GCSE history exam at Bolton School just after the second audition, and then had to rush back to Manchester for the third audition – all on the same day!' As well as showing what an energetic lad Max is, this also shows that even as his head was in the clouds with dreams of pop stardom, his feet were still firmly on the ground. Having faced the upset of his football hopes being shattered by injury, Max was making sure he had qualifications to fall back on in case his pop dreams were also to be unfulfilled. This was very sensible thinking from the young man.

"I love Elvis, Stevie Wonder and Otis Redding. The newer artists I like are Michael Jackson and Oasis."

However, Max is the first to admit that he has made mistakes along the way. He was ill-prepared for the notorious 'boot camp' stage of *The X Factor* – and he paid the price. The boot camp phase sees the acts who got through the initial judges' auditions put through an uncompromising set of intense auditions and tasks. The judges make brutal cuts after each round. Max's age category was allotted to Louis Walsh, who took them to north London's Arts Depot, which is based in north Finchley. On the first day the hopefuls had to stand on the stage in groups of ten and sing one of five songs selected by Walsh. They were then given a song to learn overnight and then allowed just one chance to perform it. 'He originally thought he could sing any song he wanted to at the boot camp,' explained his father Mark. 'He found out two days before that he had to sing one of five songs though. He wasn't comfortable with any of the songs and didn't really take the time to practise. It was a real learning curve for him and he realized straight away what he had done wrong.' He had indeed got it wrong, and he was sent home at the boot camp stage after putting in a disappointing performance in front of the judges.

Max showed his philosophical side yet again when he looked back over his *X Factor* experience. 'I didn't think I would get past the first audition of *X Factor* and to do as well as I did has really given me the confidence to carry on singing,' he said shortly after his elimination. 'If I'd done more practice I might have been able to get even further. This really could be the start of something big for me.'

However, it was not to be the last that *The X Factor* would see of Max. Indeed, he was not the only rejected contestant that year to subsequently make it big. A young lady called Alexandra Burke was also sent home by Louis Walsh, and she returned three years later to win the contest and become a huge pop sensation. For the time being, though, Max had to watch from the sidelines as another contestant from his category – Shayne Ward – won *The X Factor* and grabbed the all-important record deal. 'That's my goal,' sang Ward in his victory song. Max's goal continued to burn inside him, despite his disappointment.

He would soon find a new avenue for his fiery ambition ...

▶▶▶ 2 TOM PARKER

Full name: Tom Parker
Hometown: Bolton
Date of birth: 4 August 1988
Star sign: Leo
Height: 5'10"
Eyes: hazel
Hair: brown
Favourite food: Indian and
    Italian
Favourite band: Oasis
Football team: Bolton Wanderers
Favourite animal: parrot
Favourite TV show: *The
    Inbetweeners*

One day, when he was sixteen years of age, Tom Parker picked up a guitar. It was a moment that completely changed his life and ultimately propelled him onto the course that saw him join The Wanted. He had never really been interested in music until then. 'I even went through school without singing at all,' he said, overstating the case slightly, but still giving a flavour of his childhood. However, once he started learning some basic chords and strumming patterns, and then some songs, Tom's guitar quickly became his 'best friend'. A friend that led him to a career which would make him massively famous, lifting him to a new life he could never have imagined just a few years previously. He looks back and says: 'My guitar pretty much changed my life. Wherever I am, I just pick it up and start playing.' It was in that moment that he realized that he wanted to be a singer and musician.

Thomas Anthony Parker was born on 4 August 1988. So what sort of guy is he? 'Tom – he's just a lad from Bolton,' is how his band-mate Max describes him. But there's so much more to this remarkable young man, as we shall see. On the day Tom was born, the number one hit in Britain was the Yazz song 'The Only Way Is Up'. It's a positive, ambitious motto that Tom has tried his best to stick to throughout his life. On the same day, at the top of the album charts was a *Now That's What I Call Music* compilation. It is fitting; the album's title could almost be a mission statement for the recent years of his life, if not the first sixteen years of it. Tom was a sweet, if on occasion slightly cheeky, child. As he grew up he enjoyed sitting in front of the television. His favourite children's television show was *Rosie & Jim*, which features two ragdolls who travel the waterways of England in a narrow-boat called The Ragdoll. 'I used to watch it on TV every morning, then watch the same video every night,' he admitted of his love of the show. It's a strange, but harmless, addiction for a pop star to admit to!

Tom has always been a person who can become easily bored. Therefore, even as a little boy he was always on the lookout for something to distract himself with. He was also an untidy child growing up, something his Wanted bandmates would insist has not changed a bit, though as we have already seen, Max does on occasion rival Tom in the untidiness stakes. When the band all moved in together they quickly lost two sets of housecleaners in succession, so the mess they created was presumably formidable! Certainly Tom and Max are the chief rubbish-creators if you listen to their band-mates. According to Nathan, on 'some days' Tom's feet can become oppressively smelly, too. As for Tom, he dubs himself as 'the cheeky one in the band – hopefully!'

THE WANTED

Cheeky Tom was born under the star sign of Leo. As such, he is expected to have many traits that come in handy for a lad in his profession – creativity and enthusiasm being two dominant qualities that Leos are said to have in abundance.

Certainly the party animal, energetic Tom has demonstrated plenty of both. Leos are also said to be attracted to career paths that put them in the centre of attention. Again, this rings very true in Tom's case: he is comfortable onstage in front of audiences of thousands. It is also said that Leo men have abundant sex appeal and a romantic side, two things that Tom's many fans will be delighted to confirm. Other famous Leos include Rolling Stones legend Mick Jagger, as well as actors Ben Affleck and Arnold Schwarzenegger, who has moved from acting to politics.

"My guitar pretty much changed my life."

Like three of the other Wanted members, Tom is a big football fan. For him, there is only one team in the world worth discussing – Bolton Wanderers. The club, also known as 'The Trotters', or simply 'Wanderers', have not enjoyed major silverware or success during Tom's life, but he remains a loyal fan through good times and bad. Other famous Bolton fans include television presenter Vernon Kay and

McFly front-man Danny Jones. Tom is sure that he 'out-fans' them though, and fancies himself as a true, dyed-in-the-wool Bolton fan. Football really gets his blood pumping and he has relished the famous, noble victories that the club has enjoyed over more successful opponents in the time he has been following the beautiful game. He admits he is not a fantastic player, though. When asked what he would do if he were not in the band, he said that the answer would be 'a footballer' – were it not for the fact that, as he admits, he would not have been good enough to make it as a professional. He says he would have been more likely to be a 'bin man' or a photographer.

As a kid, he did enjoy singing for a while, including at his primary school, where he sweetly sang along in assembly and music lessons. However, as he became a teenager Tom sang less and less. 'I've always sung, but when you get to secondary school it gets a bit un-cool,' he said. That could very easily have been that for Tom's musical career. But he was urged to keep up the music by someone close to home. 'My big brother encouraged me to pick up a guitar and it just went from there,' explained Tom.

It was to be something of a life-changing moment. As he has since admitted on the band's 'Formspring' webpage (an online question and answer forum), he did not at first know how to take his musical ambitions forward. 'I always wanted to be in music but didn't really know how,' he said. This would change in time, most notably when he turned to the advertisements page of *The Stage* newspaper one fateful day.

When Tom looks back to his childhood, he is reminded of the many scars he picked up as a young whippersnapper. He has one just above his nose, from where he ripped a chicken pox blister off his face. 'It bled for ages,' he remembered. There is another scar just above his right eyebrow, from when he ran through a patio window, 'and it smashed'. He added: 'I thought it was open – stupid child!' He has one above his left eyebrow too, from when he fell off a

twittertwittertwittertwittertwittertwittertwittertwittertwittertwittertwittertwitter

TomTheWanted I'm thinking of asking JLS to be their 5th member … [Joke.]

5:17 PM Aug 16th via ÜberTwitter

rocking horse. There's yet another scar on his right cheek, 'from when I got sliced open playing football'. 'I've been in the wars,' he said, summing up his scars. Since joining the band, Tom has been accident-prone in other ways. During an interview on German television he smashed his teeth against the microphone, and, as we have seen, he managed to burn his nipple while celebrating The Wanted's first number one hit. That's Tom for you, always on the edge of a minor mishap.

THE WANTED

It was at this point Tom realized that, as well as having a flair for playing the guitar, he also had a fantastic voice. It was indie and rock bands that had the most profound effect on Tom back then. 'People like Stereophonics and Liam Gallagher had a big influence on me. I've got a really throaty, rock voice. I'm glad I never had any singing lessons – they try to teach you a certain way. I just kinda taught myself.'

twittertwittertwittertwittertwittertwittertwittertwittertwittertwittertwittertwitter

TomTheWanted England are officially awful ... full stop! [During the Football World Cup]

9:22 PM Jun 18th via ÜberTwitter

His feathery hairstyle is reminiscent of some of the cuts that Liam Gallagher has sported down the years. As well as enjoying the music of these more contemporary acts, Tom is also a major fan of The Beatles, the band who did more to influence bands like Oasis than any other. Indeed, both Gallagher brothers admit to being obsessed with the music of The Beatles. In common with Noel and Liam, Tom's favourite member of the legendary rock band is the late John Lennon. If he could be granted one wish, Tom says, it would be to meet Lennon, who was tragically murdered in New York in 1980. Tom is also a fan of the drummer of The Corrs, Caroline Corr. Though his ideal celebrity woman would be either Miley Cyrus or Rosie Jones.

Tom attended the Thornleigh Salesian College in Bolton. It is a Roman Catholic school, in which religious values play a large part. As the school's prospectus proudly states: '[Our aim is] to develop self esteem and to understand and live moral lives based on Gospel values of love, peace, justice and personal responsibility'. Other famous musicians have attended Thornleigh, including Damon Gough (who is better known by his pop moniker Badly Drawn Boy) and Danny Jones, the celebrated lead singer of successful pop/rock band McFly. The example Jones and his band set has been one that has not been lost on Tom, or any other member of The Wanted. They want every bit of the success that McFly have enjoyed – and then some more, ideally! With his feathered mop, Tom looks not unlike a member of the McFly entourage himself.

Even back in the day, long before he auditioned for The Wanted, Tom had his sights set high. 'Through school I always said that a nine-to-five job wasn't for me and my mum was always really supportive of me wanting to be in the music industry,' he said. 'I always set my sights on it but I never imagined it would happen quite so quickly.' Indeed, the theme that runs through the stories of all members of The Wanted is just how quickly they have all enjoyed success. They have sprinted their way to the front of the pack, and their fans hope that now they are there the band can take up a more marathon-like pace that sees them develop a lasting career akin to that enjoyed by the likes of McFly and Westlife.

THE WANTED

As Tom said, he was always supported in his ambitions as he grew up. One of the first steps to fame he took came when he joined a Take That tribute band, in which he got his first real taste of life in a pop group. Although this was a novelty act, it still taught him things about the dynamics of a band. 'I was Mark,' he laughed, referring to his position as the Mark Owen of the band. 'I gained a lot of experience — now I can go up on stage without being nervous.' The band was called Take That 2. 'All four of the artists have studied every detail of their character in depth,' said the publicity material for the band. 'So when you see them you really feel like you are watching the genuine thing!'

Take That 2's MySpace profile billed Tom as 'Tom "snack-a-jack" Parker' and promised of the band: 'The voice, look and mannerisms are quite simply outstanding! With no expense spared, and no corners cut, this really is the most professional tribute show package available today!'

"I gained a lot of experience — now I can go up on stage without being nervous."

Grainy YouTube footage shows them performing at Rockingham Speedway in 2008, belting out a harmonious version of 'Rule The World'. These performances were sharp learning curves for Tom and what he learnt then continues to help him to this day when he and his Wanted band-mates take to the stage for another exciting performance. He also learned how to best exist within a band – by not having a big ego. 'We're not divas and like, "I wanna be leader",' he has said of The Wanted. 'Do you know what I mean?'

Like his fellow Wanted member Max, Tom decided to try *The X Factor* route in his quest for musical fame.

twittertwittertwittertwittertwittertwittertwittertwittertwittertwittertwittertwitter

TomTheWanted Benidorm … what a place!

3:02 PM Jun 20th via ÜberTwitter

However, unlike Max, Tom was far from successful. He did not even make it through to the auditions proper. Instead he got no further than the pre-auditions in front of the show's production team. 'I just thought I might as well go for it,' he said looking back. 'My confidence was really knocked after I went on *The X Factor*. I was trying out for a solo career but looking back I was not great and I do believe it was for the best. I didn't even get to see Simon Cowell. A producer just told me to leave during the first round.' That producer might well be kicking him or herself now, as they watch the lad they rejected sitting pretty at the top of the pop tree.

Tom was once asked on the band's Formspring page whether if it were a choice between being rich, or being in the band, which he would choose. 'Rich!! Hahaha!' he replied. 'No, definitely in the band, we all would!' In time, this will be less of a choice as the band becomes more wealthy.

What more can one say about Tom to give a flavour of him? He loves eating Indian food, as long as the dish does not contain any fish. He hates fish, and alludes mysteriously to 'bad memories' of it. Sounds like a fishy tale, doesn't it? He also enjoys a few drinks, a chat and a laugh with friends. If he could play any part in any film he would be Jack Sparrow in *Pirates of the Caribbean* – mostly to co-star with Keira Knightley. Not that she's the only celebrity he fancies, he is also an admirer of Frankie Sandford from The Saturdays – but then who isn't?

Jay has complained that Tom 'stinks out The Wanted house with his poos'. But how did Tom get from a normal person, stinking out a normal house, to the famous guy he is now? He was claiming job-seekers' allowance and wondering what might happen to him in his life one minute. Then, one day, he opened *The Stage* newspaper and flicked to the advertisements section. He saw one notice for a forthcoming audition. He decided to go along and see what it was all about …

twittertwittertwittertwittertwittertwittertwittertwittertwittertwittertwittertwitter

TomTheWanted (On wheelchair basketball) Hmm I don't think I was supposed to get out of the wheelchair … but the excitement was too much! Lol.

1:31 PM Aug 29th via ÜberTwitter

▶▶▶ 3 SIVA KANESWARAN

Full name: Siva Kaneswaran
Hometown: Dublin
Date of birth: 16 November 1988
Star sign: Scorpio
Height: 6'1"
Eyes: brown
Hair: black
Favourite food: stew,
    brownies, shepherd's pie
    (not all together)
Favourite band: Switchfoot
Football team: Manchester City
    or Bolton
Favourite animal: dog
Favourite TV show: *Family Guy*

In the families of Max and Tom, there were few clues to suggest that there might be entertainment genes in the blood. In the Kaneswaran clan the opposite is true – Siva's family is bursting with show-business aspiration. 'My family is very musical, everyone can play something or sing, or both, so when this opportunity came along it was sort of the next step,' says Siva of his nearest and dearest. However, like Tom, it took him a while before he realized that he too wanted to pursue a musical future. Indeed, just like Tom, it was as a sixteen-year-old, when Siva picked up a guitar for the first time, that he was set on that path. First, though, he lived out his formative years in a most remarkable and interesting Irish family ...

Siva was born in Dublin on 16 November 1988, one of twin brothers in a large clan. His brother is named Kumar, and though they are often referred to as identical twins, Siva insists: 'We're not totally identical'. There were eight children in the Kaneswaran household – Siva, Gail, Hazel, Daniel, Kelly, David, Trevor and Kumar – but although there were a lot of them, his is a close-knit family. He suspects that the size of his family gave him the edge psychologically. 'Maybe I get the confidence coming from such a big family. We're all very supportive of each other,' he said. 'I think that gives you an inner confidence.'

They grew up in the Corduff area of Blanchardstown in County Fingal. Corduff is a place that is routinely described as 'notorious' in the media. The people are poor and the streets are often rough and dangerous. Drug abuse is rife. It is a testament to Siva and his family that they avoided getting into any trouble. The worst memory of the area Siva has was the day he was attacked with soup. 'Oh my God. Last time I was there, before I actually went into The George [pub] I got "souped",' he said. 'It was a "drive-by souping". I can't remember whether it was racial slurs or name-calling, but someone drives by, and they throw a pot of soup on you, and it's called a "drive-by souping". Bizarreness!'

Siva has had a hard life in many ways, though. In 1995, when he was just six years of age he faced the heartbreak of the totally unexpected death of his father. One day, while in a local take-away restaurant, Siva's father suffered a fatal heart attack. Mr Kaneswaran Sr was originally from Singapore and worked as a window cleaner. Although his was one of very few non-white faces in the local area, he was, according to one of Siva's sisters, 'a massively popular local figure'. A very handsome man, his good looks are just one of the legacies he left his offspring. He was a lover of soul music and passed this passion on to his children. However, he was not seeking to create a family of entertainers. Indeed, one family friend was quoted in the

twittertwittertwittertwittertwittertwittertwittertwittertwittertwittertwittertwitter
SivaTheWanted I like positive people

6:07 PM Sep 15th via TweetDeck

newspaper suggesting that all was not rosy between the father and his many children. 'There was never really a great relationship with the dad,' claimed the unnamed source in *The Mail on Sunday* newspaper. 'He was a bit of a messer, and the girls used to get upset when talking about him. He wasn't around an awful lot and he was fond of the drink. But they were all ridiculously close with the mum.'

"Maybe I get the confidence coming from such a big family."

After Siva's father died, his sisters helped their Irish mother, Lily, to raise the younger children. Lily – her actual name is Elizabeth but she is rarely called it – is a wonderful and formidable woman with red hair, whose celebrated Sunday roasts are admired by all those who have sampled

twittertwittertwittertwittertwittertwittertwittertwittertwittertwittertwitter

SivaTheWanted It's too cold in my room to get out of bed.

10:29 AM Sep 20th via Twitterrific

them. With the help of her two eldest daughters – Hazel and Gail – Lily held the family together as they coped with the trauma of her husband's sudden tragic death. What with that and the poverty that faced them, they could have been forgiven for collapsing under the weight of such challenges. But far from that, many of Lily's children have gone on to pursue – with some success – some exciting career paths. They are not quite the Jackson family, but they are certainly a remarkable clan – and Siva is far from the only ambitious member of it. Siva's sister Hazel became a singer and his other sister Gail became a model. She was the face of Dublin's celebrity nightclub Cocoon for a while, and became friendly with the club's famous owner, Eddie Irvine. An honest, straight-to-the-point woman, she describes modelling as 'smiling for a living'.

The two children who chose not to seriously chase fame are Siva's brothers Daniel and Kelly. Siva's other brother Trevor is an aspiring singer-songwriter, who is also on the books of an Irish modelling agency. In 2009 Trevor entered *The X*

Factor and made it to the latter stages of the competition. 'We used to slag him saying he learned to sing before he could talk, as he has been at it since he was three years old, when he went in for this local talent show and he won it,' said his mother. 'It's all he has ever wanted to do,' she continued. 'He really wants to make it big, and who wouldn't want to be in a programme like *The X Factor*? Ever since Hazel was in *Popstars*, our whole family has been mad about the show and we always watch it.' A friend of the family describes Trevor as, 'not just stupidly good-looking but also extremely talented musically. He is also just a really nice guy. But the whole family are like that. People really like them.'

Trevor's work had a knock-on effect for Siva, who confirmed, 'I've been writing songs with my older brother Trevor ... for years.' Siva too has done some modelling, as he explained to *Attitude*, the gay magazine. 'I did a shoot for Gareth Pugh. It was in *i-D*, and I wore this massive ball thingy on my shoulders, but it was huge! It went above my head and it was full of bull hair. I was wearing some kind of Japanese sandals with the tightest glittery pants on ... and I had no top on.'

As the siblings chased their respective channels of fame, they were also always there to support one another. When sister Hazel entered the talent show called *Popstars: The Rivals* in 2002 she was a real hit with the judging panel of Louis Walsh, Geri Halliwell and Pete Waterman. Consequently, she went far in the contest. However, she was heavily pregnant during the key stages of the competition and had to drop out.

In the end, the girl band launched from that contest – Girls Aloud – have since gone on to become a pop sensation. Hazel must watch their success and wonder what could have been. This was a disappointment in a different league to that of Max, as he watched Eton Road progress in the live finals of *The X Factor* after his band Avenue had been eliminated in their favour.

Hazel remains philosophical, though. 'You'd be a liar if you said you didn't envy Girls Aloud,' she said. 'But I also have four kids so I have big experiences as a mother they [the Girls Aloud members] don't have yet.'

Hazel has since become a steady and guiding hand in Siva's career, while still enjoying success herself. In the wake of her *Popstars* disappointment Hazel released a solo single, 'Heartbreak Valley', which became Ireland's entry in the World Song Competition, which is a competition similar to the Eurovision Song Contest. Hazel went on to have three top ten solo hits in Ireland. She also became something of a television personality there for a while, with appearances on everything from RTÉ's comedy panel show *The Panel* to the Meteor Music Awards. She was even a judge on RTÉ's talent show *You're a Star*.

THE WANTED

Another of Siva's siblings, David, who describes himself as 'spiritual, inquisitive and very un-materialistic', was a founding member of an Irish boy band called Zoo. The band's official website describes them as 'a hard edge pop

twittertwittertwittertwittertwittertwittertwittertwittertwittertwittertwitter

SivaTheWanted My life is complete when I have brownies to eat. Oh ye. http://plixi.com/p/43930800

2:26 PM Sep 8th via ÜberTwitter

band with a massive rock-inspired twist'. In 2005 they peaked in popularity and played a back-breaking number of concerts all around Ireland. They have supported Irish pop giants Westlife in huge arenas and stadiums. They were also special guests on a tour by former Westlife solo artist Brian McFadden. Their second single 'I Wanna Be Your Lover' made some waves in the pop charts. David looks back fondly on family Christmases in which he, Siva and the rest of the clan would gather round the fire and sing Jackson Five tunes. Meanwhile, Siva's twin Kumar has also had a crack at the fame game including – as we shall see – an audition for The Wanted.

In one of those 'small world' moments, Siva was a fan of a local singer called Una Healy. 'I used to listen to her songs on MySpace because I listened to all kinds of music and I was only a kid when I first met her,' he told an Irish newspaper. 'Una knows my sisters because when you're on the Dublin scene everyone knows you as it's really only a village.' Una is now part of the smash-hit British girl group The Saturdays, who share the same management as The Wanted.

As for Siva, he watched his siblings' quest for fame with interest. He was particularly impressed by Hazel's talent and determination, which influenced him to follow in her footsteps, though he also tried the same route as Gail. 'I fell in love with music and doing singing through Hazel, and I also tried modelling because of Gail,' he revealed. 'What I really wanted was singing and now it has all clicked in.'

"I fell in love with music and doing singing through Hazel ..."

What a remarkable family. A tough one, too, according to those who know them. 'The family are not aggressive but, with the exception of David, who really is very gentle, they are incredibly tough. Come on, they're from Corduff!' Indeed, as Siva insists, he and his twin brothers are not just tough people, but hard workers. 'We weren't spoilt, though; we were like the Cinderellas of the family, always doing the work!' he told *OK!* magazine. 'We're identical twins, and people do mix us up. We used to do modelling together but I wasn't keen on it, I was looking to get into singing. Kumar's still modelling, and he's going to college too. He's getting a proper education!'

THE WANTED

Siva is a particularly popular member of The Wanted, due to his stunning good looks. Many of the band's fans dream of dating him. However, he is not – at the time of writing – available. He met a girl some time ago, who continued to be his girlfriend once he found fame with The Wanted. 'I'm the only one with a girlfriend,' he told *OK!* magazine. 'Her name's Nareesha. We met a long time ago in Belfast. She's a shoe designer and she's from Jay's hometown of Nottingham. When I started out in The Wanted, it was quite difficult for us, but I think she realizes that I have to put a lot of time into the band.'

So there we have the back-story of the third member of The Wanted. There are just two more to go ...

twittertwittertwittertwittertwittertwittertwittertwittertwittertwittertwitter

SivaTheWanted This mornin I had a real urge to sky dive!! Like a big urge. God, what is wrong with me. Lol.

11:29 AM Sep 14th via ÜberTwitter

▶▶▶ 4 JAY MCGUINESS

Full name: James McGuiness
Hometown: Nottingham
Date of birth: 24 July 1990
Star sign: Leo
Height: 6'1"
Eyes: blue
Hair: brown
Favourite food: pizza, pasta with
pesto, chips, cheese toasties,
Starbars, eggs in any form
Favourite bands: Coldplay,
Newton Faulkner, Florence,
Jack Penate, Damien Rice
Football team: Celtic
Favourite animal: chimp
Favourite TV show: anything
with David Attenborough,
Misfits

J ames 'Jay' McGuiness was born in Nottingham on 24 July 1990, making him a Leo, like his band-mate Tom. Jay grew up in Farndon, a small village a couple of miles south-west of Newark, on the banks of the River Trent. It is a sweet area, which once had the benefit of a ferry that ran across the River Trent to nearby Rolleston. It was a nice place to grow up in, with a great deal of charm and character. Jay, as he soon became known to those close to him, enjoyed some happy formative years there. He is indeed very much a homebody – until he joined The Wanted he had rarely strayed away from the region in which he grew up. During his teenage years he and his family moved to Carlton, a suburb to the east of the city of Nottingham.

Like his Wanted band-mate Siva, Jay has a twin brother, called Tom. (Another thing that Siva and Jay have in common is their height.) Jay told *Metro* that he and his twin brother had never had any freaky, psychic experiences. 'We were both sick on the bus at the same time on our first day of school, though,' he added. 'We're not identical twins. That "psychic twin" stuff is just because you've had the same lives growing up. It's a load of rubbish.' If Jay and his brothers were big kids, Jay was a particularly fun-loving one. As a child, his favourite television show was *How 2*, which starred brain-box television personality Carol Vorderman, of *Countdown* fame. In the show, Carol taught young viewers a series of facts and tricks with which to impress their friends. Jay was gripped and impressed. 'Carol Vorderman – is there anything you didn't teach us?' he once asked, rhetorically. The programme appealed to the show-off side of Jay's nature. Nowadays, of course, he has found a better way of showing off, and the audiences are considerably bigger and noisier. He also enjoyed watching nature television documentaries, and continues to do so. 'Anything with David Attenborough,' he said when recently asked what his favourite sort of television is. Perhaps in keeping with his love of animals, Jay is a vegetarian.

Unlike his Wanted band-mates, Jay is not a major football fan. When asked who he supports, he replied, 'Celtic, at a push, I rarely watch footy'. This made him something of an oddity within his family. Everyone else in the household is mad about the beautiful game – even his mother! All three of his brothers and sisters are big football fans and his mother was the captain of the local women's team! 'I was just so bad at it!' he said. 'I used to sit at home eating crisps and watching telly while they were all out at footie.' As we shall see, he was to receive occasional unpleasant remarks from some other kids because of his lack of interest in the game.

THE WANTED

For Jay, music and performing has always been his first love. He attended a suitable school, given that creativity and the arts are his passion. All Saints' School, Mansfield has a very creative edge to its curriculum. The school's current head teacher, Mr Cobbett, describes the establishment as 'a lively, Catholic comprehensive school with a very special, warm ethos which is recognized by all who visit.' Cobbett adds: 'It has been a Performing Arts College since 2002 and music, dance and drama are very strong within the school with all students getting the opportunity to take part in a variety of musical and dramatic performances.'

"He was an excellent pupil and I am so proud . . . "

It is also a school where religion is important to both teachers and pupils. As the school's prospectus explains, two of its aims are 'putting God at the centre of our community' and 'practising our Christian responsibilities towards the wider community and our environment'.

It was, therefore, a balanced education and experience for Jay at All Saints' School. He fell in love with dancing quite by the chance, at the age of thirteen. Around this time, Jay's mother was attending a dance class and one day he decided to tag along with her. He loved what he saw. It made him come alive inside. He began to dance himself, and quickly found it was easy to perfect. 'It was the only thing I was ever good at,' he said. 'I really got obsessed with it.'

A tall, lively and fun boy, he is remembered by many who encountered him at All Saints'. 'When he first came to the school James was really talented,' said Assistant Head Mrs Chris Young. 'He was an excellent pupil and I am so proud and I wish them all the success in the world.' His former class-mates are just as pleased for Jay, now he is a well-known pop star. Megan Smith was a school friend of Jay's and says that no matter how famous he becomes she will always remember him the same way. She said: 'Although he is known as Jay in the band, he [is] still James to us.'

However, it was soon time for Jay to fly the All Saints' nest and to soar to even greater heights. When he turned sixteen, Jay left the school and joined the Midlands Academy

twittertwittertwittertwittertwittertwittertwittertwittertwittertwittertwittertwitter

JayTheWanted OK HANDS UP! I aint a gangsta!! But I've got to practice my bad ass skills for something special coming up soon …

4:11 PM Sep 7th via ÜberTwitter

of Dance and Drama (MADD) in the Carlton area of Nottingham. Jay had great fun there. The course he studied was a varied one, which involved a range of creative disciplines including musical theatre, tap, ballet, jazz, drama and singing. As he put it himself, 'It was all-singing, all-dancing, stuff like that'. Sounds '*Glee*-ful', though Jay snappily contests the comparison whenever it is made. On the whole, his family assumed that it would be in the discipline of dance that Jay would go on to carve out a career. They were surprised, though very happy, when he turned out to become a famous singer rather than dancer.

Founded in 1967, the Midlands Academy of Dance and Drama is a very well-respected institution that is an accredited course provider of the Council for Dance Education and Training. It aims to give a full and varied training to its students, as the establishment's website explains: 'In order to meet the needs of the "Theatre and TV

twittertwittertwittertwittertwittertwittertwittertwittertwittertwittertwittertwitter

JayTheWanted OK HANDS UP! I aint a gangsta!! But I've got to practice my bad ass skills for something special coming up soon …

4:11 PM Sep 7th via ÜberTwitter

in the 21st century" [course title], performers must be able to sing, dance and act, and be prepared to use their skills to the maximum in order to secure employment in the performing arts industry'. Among others who have passed through the academy's doors are Hollie Robertson, who won the second series of the BBC talent show *Strictly Dance Fever*. As for Jay, he confirmed that the academy is sometimes known by its acronym: MADD. 'Yeah, it really is called that,' he laughed. 'And no, it's nothing like *Glee*'.

Jay has often been described as 'nimble-footed'. But, while his dancing is admired by those who appreciate the art form, for others it has occasionally been something to mock him about. Coupled with the fact he is not a big fan of football, Jay's dancing perhaps inevitably attracted jibes and teasing from some as he grew up. 'I got a bit of stick when I was younger,' he explained. 'I got called Billy Elliot, as I really liked dance while everyone else was into football. They used to call me banana-kick because I couldn't manage to kick the ball in a straight line.'

Even now, a journalist interviewing Jay might stumble upon a raw nerve by asking him if it is true that he is the Billy Elliot of the band. 'Oh man, don't say that!' Jay told one. 'No way!' It is a comparison he is pleased to see the back of, now he has become more known as a member of The Wanted.

"They used to call me banana-kick because I couldn't manage to kick the ball in a straight line."

THE WANTED

After he left MADD, Jay began to attend dance auditions. These are gruelling, tough experiences. There is a whole circuit of such auditions, at many of which the same faces keep appearing again and again. The judging panel might not consist of television stars such as Simon Cowell, but they can still be exacting and harsh. There was an added complication for Jay – his musical tastes. Most auditionees loved music that tied in with the dance genre. Jay's tastes were less appropriate, as he admitted. 'Thing is I'm not like the other dancers – they were all into R & B and I'm into indie and Jack Penate, Cat Stevens, stuff like that,' he said. Who could have guessed then, as he queued up – sometimes for many hours – for a tough dance audition, that ultimately Jay would not choose dancing as a career path? Instead, he – quite literally – found his voice and decided to have a crack at a career as a pop star.

It was a very wise choice. He's not done badly so far, has he?

twittertwittertwittertwittertwittertwittertwittertwittertwittertwittertwittertwitter

JayTheWanted Ok – we met him [Robbie Williams] – properly properly starstruck. I need a sit down. He shook my hand & asked how everything's going, I mumbled some crap :S x

9:37 PM Sep 3rd via ÜberTwitter

▶ ▶ ▶ 5 NATHAN SYKES

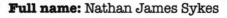

Full name: Nathan James Sykes
Hometown: Gloucester
Date of birth: 18 April 1993
Star sign: Aries
Height: 5'9"
Eyes: green/blue
Hair: brown
Favourite food: spag bol, Chinese,
    soup, roast dinners
Favourite band: Boyz II Men
Football team: Manchester
    United
Favourite animal: cat
Favourite TV show: *Match of the
Day*, *Britain's Got Talent*

As the baby of the band, Nathan has always attracted comments about how young he is to enjoy such a successful pop career. With his boyish good looks, these sorts of observations are probably inevitable. But, those who say this don't know the half of it – he was only six years old when he first stepped on to a stage to sing to an audience. As such, he has actually had a longer musical career than any of his Wanted band-mates. Indeed, Nathan believes that, despite his young years, in many ways he is actually the senior member of the group. 'I might be the youngest, but I'm a bit of an old man really,' he said. 'I just sit in the corner with me cup of tea and take it all in.' Nathan might look like a sweet little angel but as his own band-mate Max says of Nathan: 'You think he's all young and cute but actually he's really dead dry and sarcastic.'

From that debut performance as a six-year-old right up to the present day, Nathan has never stopped working. Not even the iciest of hearts could fail to melt with joy at his success. As his father Harry now says, 'I'm extremely proud of him. From my point of view, Nathan has worked tirelessly to achieve this goal ever since the age of six.' He has indeed been working tirelessly. Given his age, his cute looks and floppy hair, Nathan is often compared to the pop sensation Justin Bieber. The young Canadian first came to the public eye after he entered a singing contest held in the town he grew up in. Well, Nathan could teach Bieber a thing or two about talent contests. In his short life Nathan has already entered more than ten significant talent shows. So, by the time all that work finally paid off with his place in The Wanted, Nathan had the whole talent contest thing down to a tee.

twittertwittertwittertwittertwittertwittertwittertwittertwittertwittertwittertwitter

NathanTheWanted Just realized that I'm the only United fan in this pub from the silence that followed the United goal!!!

2:16 PM Sep 19th via ÜberTwitter

"You think he's all young and cute but actually he's really dead dry and sarcastic."

His life-story is one of relentless determination and energy. Even some of the most seasoned audition-goers and competition-enterers would feel exhausted simply reading of how many times Nathan has submitted himself to such contests. Do not be fooled by those angelic features: deep within Nathan burns a smouldering fire of determination and ambition. He is also has a very sharp mind. Early in life he had a sense that he had a special talent and that sharing it with the world was to be his vocation. When he watched performers on television he sat enraptured by them. It looked like so much fun and Nathan was keen to get a bit of that action. It did not take him long to start enjoying it.

He was born on 18 April 1993, under the star sign of Aries. Determination in the face of challenges is a leading

Arian trait, which might explain why Nathan was willing to enter so many competitions. Nathan does indeed show many of the traits of the Ram, including a willingness to gamble; after all, entering talent contests is a gamble against the tightest of odds. You rehearse, prepare and then audition, sometimes queuing for many hours. All that effort is staked on the slim chance that the panel will like what they see enough to want to see more. Arians also are believed to have great charisma, which is a quality that Nathan has in abundance. Two other musical Arians are Mariah Carey and Elton John. Where Nathan parts company with his fellow Arians is in their supposed tendency to quit a challenge if positive results are not quickly achieved. He is a young man who has shown more persistence and determination than most people his age. He has kept working and working for his dream, no matter what obstacles are placed in his way. The word 'quitter' could never be sensibly applied to Nathan, particularly when it comes to his musical ambitions.

It is not hard to see what kick-started Nathan's interest in performance and fame. Growing up, his favourite television show was *The Saturday Show*, a BBC programme first aired in 2001, when it replaced the long-running show *Live & Kicking*. Among those who have presented it – and who perhaps caught Nathan's eye even as a youngster – are glamorous girls Dani Behr and Fearne Cotton. As he watched the exciting, fun-packed show roll out each week, young Nathan dreamed of being a part of such a show himself one day. He loved the glamour and fun of it. There was comedy, energy and music – all things to which Nathan is naturally drawn. He has a wicked sense of humour, as Max and the rest of The Wanted will confirm.

Given Nathan's ambitious nature, he would not have to wait long to take part in programmes such as *The Saturday Show*, and although he might be the youngest member of The Wanted, he was the first to taste television fame.

First, though, he had school to attend. Although Nathan has never been the most enthusiastic of pupils – he says that he loves it when it snows and he does not have to go to school for a day – he nonetheless had some fun and educational times at all the establishments he attended. Those who knew Nathan at school remember him well. Some fellow students could see a certain star quality in him from the start. Others just remember him as 'cute little Nathan'. His first school was Longlevens Junior School in Gloucester. Among the stated aims of the school are 'to generate enquiring minds capable of communicating effectively (verbally, creatively and technically) with others'. The creative side of the curriculum has proved to be the most relevant to Nathan's development. Longlevens aims to let its pupils 'experience role play, imaginative play, dance, music and art, giving them the opportunity to develop their own ideas through expressing their creativity'. The school can be rightly proud of him.

Their pride was justified by the number of contests in which he starred. 'Talented drama students from Gloucester swept the board at the

Bristol Drama Festival,' reported a local newspaper in November 1999. 'Gold medals and trophies were awarded to eight youngsters aged from six to 16, for their acting dialogue, news-reading, verse speaking and mime skills.' One of the students listed was 'Nathan Sykes, six'. He and his family were so happy, as was his teacher, Mrs Chidzoy, 'I was very proud of their results. Many second and third places were also won by students who had strong competition.'

Nathan was soon proving an inspiration to his little sister Jessica, then just two-and-a-half years old. She and her three-year-old friend Emily Poole overheard their respective older brothers (Nathan and his friend Robert Poole) reciting poetry ahead of an upcoming competition. The little girls decided to have a crack at poetry-reading themselves. As their drama teacher Jacqueline Chidzoy said: 'The two boys were preparing for their poetry competitions and rehearsing the test poems at their homes when their tiny sisters ran happily around reciting the lines.' Mrs Chidzoy was impressed when they recited poetry in front of her. 'I was amazed that such little people could learn so well,' she said.

The teacher then urged the girls to enter a poetry competition at the Bristol Federation Festival in the 'five years and under' category. Jessica recited a work by Ian Hamont and Emily read a Julie Holder poem called 'Two In One'. Both girls won certificates, and Jessica even landed a second place award. Not bad considering her very tender years. It was Nathan, though, who stole the show in the eyes of the onlookers. 'A Gloucester theatre's finances have benefitted by youngsters from Jacqueline Chidzoy's dance and drama classes putting on a show,' a reporter from the *Gloucester Citizen* wrote. 'Students aged two to eighteen performed in Jackie and Friends Entertain at the Olympus Theatre, whose funds were swelled by the takings … The opening act was six-year-old Nathan Sykes with an energetic song-and-dance routine.'

THE WANTED

The following year, as a seven-year-old, he began to play piano, though he insists that he was not particularly good at playing. 'I've got to say I was absolutely shocking. My little sister was much better,' he said. He was shockingly good as a singer, though. In October 2000, he took part in a contest called the Massive Millennium Showcase. The final was held at the Cheltenham and Gloucester College of Higher Education, watched by town mayor Councillor Daphne Pennell. Nathan was described by the *Gloucestershire Echo* as 'the star of the show'. The newspaper reported that he 'bounced, flounced and skipped across stage like his hero Robbie Williams. Clutching the microphone tightly to his lips, the seven-year-old delivered "A Deeper Shade Of Blue" by Steps.' Nathan received the noisiest applause from the excited audience. He told the local newspaper: 'I learn the words to songs by listening to CDs and I've got a tape of boy band music which I sing too.' He won the People's Choice award, and left the venue with the Massive Millennium Shield and theatre passes worth £100.

Nathan's local fame was increasing apace – and his proud parents were also enjoying their moment in the limelight. 'Nathan is a talent to watch,' declared the *Gloucester Citizen* the next day. His father was quoted in the report. 'Nathan's really chuffed,' said proud Harry. 'He didn't think he'd win. We told him just to enjoy it and he went along and did his best. At the end of the day the judges saw his personality come through, the way he kept eye contact and smiled all the time. He really enjoyed it.'

He was indeed a talent to watch. In the months after this victory he also performed at the Grand Gala Showcase at Cheltenham's Bacon Theatre and sang at the fortieth wedding anniversary party of a local couple, at which he helped raise funds for Children In Need. What a wonderful time Nathan was having performing – and what fun his audiences were having as a result.

twittertwittertwittertwittertwittertwittertwittertwittertwittertwittertwittertwitter

NathanTheWanted Derren Brown … I wonder if I'm the next target?!

11:15 PM Sep 8th via ÜberTwitter

By the time he was eight, Nathan was expressing his creativity in front of a television audience, when he appeared on a BBC One talent show called *Britney Spears' Karaoke Kriminals*. It was a strangely named contest, but young Nathan took the plunge and got the reward – finishing the show as the winner! He had been the only male in the contest and he was also the smallest entrant. As the winner he got a trophy, a signed photograph of Britney Spears and a skirt she had worn in a pop video. Perhaps more exciting than any of that was that he also got a kiss from Ms Spears herself, who was at the televised final.

'He's so cute,' said Britney, as she handed Nathan his prizes. 'He was very good.' Presenter Dani Behr, whom Nathan had watched agog on the television just a few years earlier, asked him what he would do with Britney's skirt. 'I'm going to frame it and put it on my wall,' he said, adding that he would *not* be trying it on … His kiss from Britney had been quite a moment, though. 'She said I was adorable. I was only eight and totally star-struck, but thought

I'd ask for a kiss and she gave me one on the cheek. I was a hero for years at school.'

"She said I was adorable. I was only eight and totally star-struck."

What an experience it had been. During the recording, he and the other finalists had met many star acts, including Blue, Destiny's Child and S Club 7. 'I really enjoyed it and Britney was really nice,' said Nathan. 'It felt great to win. I can't believe I did, as all the other finalists were very good indeed. We all got on really well and it's been excellent.' Best of all, though, his confidence had increased as a result of this triumph. Even at such a young age, having rubbed shoulders on a television show with already famous stars, Nathan got a handy taste of life in the spotlight – and he liked it.

His mother Karen was happy too. As she said: 'We all had a brilliant time and we are so pleased he won. We were looked after really well and the people from the BBC were brilliant with the children. Funnily enough he is dancing in a Britney Spears tribute show at the Everyman in Cheltenham next week and really looking forward to it.'

"I was nervous the first time I had to do a competition."

THE WANTED

However, Nathan's talents and passions were varied. In that same year he won a prize at the Cheltenham Festival, for Grade 2 verse and prose speaking. He was becoming unstoppable in his ambitions and successes. Even while on holiday in Yarmouth that August he managed to pick up two further gongs. While enjoying a break at the Haven Holiday park with his family, Nathan decided to have a crack at the under-eleven junior talent and under-eleven disco-dancing competitions – and, to the delight of him and his family, he won both contests. Mum Karen said: 'We were all really pleased Nathan did so well. After winning the regional heats he is now going to the national finals.'

He won T-shirts, a certificate, mug and badges together with two caravan holidays for his family. Not bad for a quick contest while on holiday! 'I was nervous the first time I had to do a competition, but have got a bit more used to it now,' he said. 'It was really good fun.' His mum added: 'To win two competitions is fantastic, especially when you think he was competing against children three years older than him.'

Never a complacent lad, Nathan made sure he was always striving to improve himself. The weekly classes he was taking in various disciplines – singing lessons with Michael Clifton, street dancing with Nikki Dawn Coady and dance lessons with Jacqueline Chidzoy – were truly paying off. The next contest in which he took part was the breakfast television show *GMTV*'s 'Tot Stars' competition, where he beat off competition from 6,000 other entrants to win a place in the quarter-finals at the Glades Shopping Centre in Bromley, Kent. The two songs he chose to sing were 'Deeper Shade of Blue' by Steps and 'Evergreen' by *Pop Idol* winner Will Young. 'It was great fun, and the audience got really enthusiastic, especially when the judges arrived,' said Nathan.

Three years later and he was back on television. This time the youngster, by now eleven years of age, entered an *X Factor*-style competition on the Saturday morning kids' show *Ministry Of Mayhem*. It provided him with yet more television experience and exposure. In 2002 he competed in a leading youth dance contest, which was being held in Montell's nightclub in Tewkesbury. He was dressed up in a costume reminiscent of the Village People, complete with a black leather cap and fingerless gloves.

In the spring of 2004, Nathan won a scholarship to attend the well-known and prestigious Sylvia Young Theatre School in London. As the actors' bible *The Stage* reported from the ceremony: 'Nathan Sykes, aged ten, was presented with the Emma Priest Scholarship for musical theatre. The award, which is in its third year, is presented in memory of the promising young performer who trained at the school and went on to make her West End debut aged sixteen in the revival of *Stop the World – I Want to Get Off*. Priest was regarded as one of the brightest young stars of musical theatre when she passed away aged just twenty-nine in 2002.'

"It was great fun, and the audience got really enthusiastic."

The Sylvia Young Theatre School was first opened in 1981. It was based in London's Drury Lane, though it moved to Marylebone two years later. It has since become such a phenomenal success story that Young was given an OBE in 2005. Among those who have been taught there are Amy Winehouse, McFly lead singer Tom Fletcher, Spice Girl

Emma Bunton, Busted member Matt Willis and All Saints sisters Natalie and Nicole Appleton. No wonder it has such a fine name, for successive generations of pop fans it has been key in providing talent.

Nathan was delighted to win a place at the school and speaks highly of his time at Sylvia Young. From the very start he showed his dedication by the sheer length of journey he regularly made from his home in Gloucester to the school in London. It was a long trip, meaning a very early start. This did not go unnoticed at the school. 'They used to think here comes the nutter that gets up at five every morning,' he said. Now that is dedication.

Then in 2004 Nathan was again competing in a television competition, this time the Junior Eurovision Song Contest. Just eleven years old, he performed a self-written song called 'Born To Dance'. He finished third out of eight contestants – a respectable showing from the youngster.

twittertwittertwittertwittertwittertwittertwittertwittertwittertwittertwittertwitter

NathanTheWanted We just had massive water fight in the car with @jaynecollinsmac … She lost.

5:30 PM Sep 7th via ÜberTwitter

Perhaps a seed for future success was sewn here, because Jayne Collins, who was then the Eurovision casting company, would one day be The Wanted's band manager.

By this time he had left the Sylvia Young Theatre School and was attending a new school in Gloucester – Ribston Hall. Although in the main a girls' school, Ribston Hall allows boys to join the mixed-gender sixth form, where there are over 250 students. It is a school with a creative bent, shown by its statement: 'Commitment to, and involvement in, extra-curricular musical activities is expected'. Here, Nathan continued his musical education and further honed his abilities in singing, dancing and other areas. It should be noted that Nathan is a musical maestro across many disciplines: he even loves playing the bagpipes. 'I've played for years,' he said. 'I just love performing.'

He would get to do a whole load more of that when he joined what quickly became Britain's most sensational boy band. First, though, we have some unfinished business to tie up with Max …

▶▶ 6 THE MAX FACTOR

When we left Max, he was dusting himself down after his knock-back from *The X Factor*. He bounced back quickly. First, he arranged to record a 'demo' CD of his singing, to distribute round record labels, talent scouts and managers. He also had ambitions to audition for parts in Hollywood movies. One such ambition was for a part in the film *Notes on a Scandal*. Based on the novel of the same name, *Notes on a Scandal* tells the story of a young female art teacher who has a scandalous affair with a fifteen-year-old male pupil. Naturally, given the sensational storyline, the film was controversial, and it became a hit upon its release, partly due to the presence in its cast of the legendary actress Dame Judi Dench. Max came within a whisker of a part in the cast himself, but it was ultimately not to be.

Perhaps the next move for Max might be another tilt at *The X Factor*, speculated his prescient father in an interview with a local newspaper. In the wake of Max's exit from the show he spoke of his pride for what his son had already achieved as well as his hopes for the future. 'I'm really proud of what Max is doing and he really does have the world at his feet,' said Mark. 'He's throwing his efforts into every area at the moment and hoping that something works out for him.' Looking ahead, Mark added: 'If he's still looking for a break when the next *X Factor* auditions are held then he'll definitely have another go. The judges were all really pleased with him and Simon said Max reminded him of Robbie Williams. He'll be one year older next time and will have improved so hopefully he'll go even further in the competition.'

He did indeed have another go. The following year he was back at *The X Factor*, but this time he was auditioning as part of a group called Avenue. The genesis of the band is of added importance given that it went on to cause such controversy and heartache. 'They've been together for five months,' presenter Kate Thornton declared when she introduced their audition. This detail was to prove to be the subject of a contentious issue further down the line. For now, though, she simply asked them whether they thought they stood a chance of getting through to the boot camp stage of the competition. 'Yes,' said Max, his response echoed by the other band members. They had been through the customary pre-auditions in front of the producers and impressed them with their vocal harmonies and the fact that they looked and stood like a band. The rapport was evident.

For the others this was their first encounter with Mr Cowell and the rest of the famous panel, but Max had been through this experience before. On the day, he wore a yellow shirt, and he took a final sip of water before the band walked into the audition room. They appeared in front of the judges as a tight and cheerful unit, prompting smiles of approval from Sharon Osbourne. The band's charisma was definitely shining through again. 'So tell me,' she said, 'are you a boy band or a vocal group.' Max was the first band member to reply, and he kept it simple. 'We just sing together,' he said, 'and love doing it … like doing it, and try and enjoy it.'

Interestingly, in contrast to The Wanted, in which Max is the oldest member, in Avenue he was the youngest. He was indeed a full five years younger than the eldest Avenue member – Jonny Lloyd. The senior Avenue member had previously been a body-double for Blue heart-throb Duncan James, and had also danced for Girls Aloud. Scouser Andy Brown had previously been in a Beatles tribute band and had appeared on *Stars In Their Eyes* at the age of thirteen. Although older than Max, Andy admitted that he often turned to him for advice when he was down. Andy added that Max's family had also often been the source of comfort and help to him, and that Max was 'the funniest person I've ever met, he just makes me laugh'. Ross Candy was an alumnus of the Academy of Contemporary Music (ACM) in Guildford. The line-up was completed by Scott Clarke, who had received a standing ovation from Michael Jackson during a Jackson tribute show, and could also boast an appearance in the Harry Potter film franchise.

When it was time for the all-important audition performance in front of the judges, Max and his band-mates sang a wonderful harmony version of Will Young's hit 'Leave Right Now'. This was a symbolic song choice in many ways. The BRIT Award-nominated song had been a hit for Young, who is one of reality television's most successful graduates. By the same token, Avenue certainly did not want to be leaving the competition right then. It was an impressive and melodious performance in which Max was key, but the notorious Simon Cowell was fairly quick to interrupt their flow.

'Okay ... okay,' he sighed. After a pause that must have seemed excruciatingly long to Max, Cowell finally expanded his verdict. 'Look, it was okay,' he shrugged. Max was quick to speak up for the band. Sensing that Cowell might be sitting on the fence over whether to send them through, he said: 'We've not been together long, I'm sure we can get better.' As some contestants – including Will Young – have found, a bit

twittertwittertwittertwittertwittertwittertwittertwittertwittertwittertwittertwitter

MaxTheWanted Bliss shoot today! Jay has his 'face' on haha! Tom has got his Cheri Blair face goin!

11:59 AM Sep 9th via ÜberTwitter

of spoken determination can help tip the balance of the judge's decision. So this was a shrewd move on Max's part.

Perhaps it worked, because Louis Walsh then intervened to stick up for Avenue. His verdict was very important to the group, because Walsh has managed two of the most successful boy bands of all time – Boyzone and Westlife. 'They're not bad, Simon,' he said. 'I'm not saying they're bad,' agreed Cowell, as Max and his band-mates waited on-edge for the discussion to reach some sort of conclusion. It was excruciating. Walsh then added that they were somewhere between not bad and great. Osbourne then told them: 'You've got nice personalities, you all look good. I think you would scrub up well.' Cowell, though, was ready to declare his ultimate verdict. 'I don't get it,' he said, to the visible deflation of Max and his band-mates. 'I'm going to say "no".' This was a devastating blow to their chances, but thankfully both Walsh and Osbourne voted to put the band through.

'Guys,' Walsh warned them as they celebrated, 'I just hope you're not in Simon's category!' He added that they would need to prove Cowell wrong. With that specific goal ringing in their ears, Max and his band-mates ran bouncing and cheering out of the audition room. They had done it! It had been a very tense deliberation from the judges, and Cowell's disapproval was worrying, but the most important thing was that Avenue had made it through to the next round. Max was delighted. He was determined that in the latter stages of the competition he would take the process more seriously than he had when he had entered alone the previous year. On that occasion, he had been caught out; this time, he hoped and believed he would not be.

This time round there were 180 contestants chosen to perform at the boot camp stage, with the harsh reality that just twenty-one acts would go through to the next round. For Max and the other Avenue boys, this was to be a major challenge and one they were determined not to fail. Walsh had been allotted the group category, so for the second year running he was the judge that Max would be facing at the boot camp stage. Walsh took along Westlife star Kian Egan and vocal coach Yvie Burnett to help him make up his mind which of the acts he would take through to the all-important live shows. Walsh was at first distinctly unimpressed with the quality of the bands he saw. 'I saw no star acts there,' he said at the end of the first day. 'It is not looking good.' Although this boded badly for the category, it at least meant that on the second day of the boot camp Max and the rest of Avenue had a great opportunity to stand out of the pack.

Walsh quickly cut the number of bands from thirty-two to sixteen. Avenue survived this cull and their confidence rightly soared as a result. They jumped for joy every time they made it through. Still, Max was all too aware that they had to keep their feet on the ground. He couldn't cope with the thought of a second successive disappointment at the boot camp stage. Avenue remained in the competition and were through to the 'judge's house' phase of the competition. This was so exciting for them all, esepcially Max, who had now progressed further than he had the previous year.

While Cowell took his category to Miami and Osbourne took hers to the Dorchester Hotel in London, Walsh took Avenue and the rest of the bands to Ireland's gorgeous Dromoland Castle, in County Clare. The weather would not be as tropical as Miami, but the surroundings were grand. The stakes were high and so was the excitement level of Avenue. 'There are not many boy bands in the charts at the moment and we want to rectify that,' said Jamie, 'and we think we have something really different to offer.' Would Walsh agree? Initially he did. It came down in his mind to a choice between Avenue and another boy band – Eton Road. Of the latter act he had said, 'They're fresh, something new. I'm not massively disappointed. I just don't know what to do with them.' So he sent Eton Road home and sent Avenue through to the live finals. Max and the rest of Avenue were jubilant. They were through to the live shows, which attract massive television audiences. They would perform each Saturday night and then the public vote would decide their fate. How exciting for them! Or so they thought …

As it turned out, before they could even get that far, everything went wrong for Max's group. 'BAND IS AVENUE YOU ALL ON,' read a headline in *The Sun*, which heralded a controversy that would be the beginning of the end for Max's *X Factor* dream. The article revealed that music manager Ashley Tabor, of the Global Talent Group (which had previous *X Factor* stars G4 and Shayne Ward on its books) had put the band together. This contradicted the account the band themselves had given on the show – that they were friends who had formed the band themselves. It was then revealed that the show's producers were furious at this revelation and also that Tabor and Avenue had since parted company. 'We put them under contract as we believe they have a bright future,' said a spokesperson for Tabor. 'At no time did we inform the show or judges we were involved. We have since been advised the contract is outside the rules of the show. We were unaware of that. The contract has been cancelled. Avenue are no longer professionally represented.'

It all looked gloomy for Max and his band as they were summoned to meet Walsh on-camera to discuss this

twittertwittertwittertwittertwittertwittertwittertwittertwittertwittertwittertwitter

TomTheWanted LA's been amazing … but England here we come! Can't wait to see everyone x

10:27 PM Oct 30th via mobile web

revelation. 'I've just found out that Avenue have been lying to me all through the competition,' Walsh explained to the cameras. 'They told me they are friends who got together to make this band.' However, as the programme revealed, the band had in fact been put together by a manager who had previously been an *X Factor* employee but had since parted company with the show. 'It's all over the papers,' continued Walsh. 'Everybody's talking about it, everybody thinks it's a fix.' *The X Factor* thrives on twists and controversy. Clearly, the programme-makers were not about to let this sort of scandal pass quietly.

"It's all over the papers . . . everybody thinks it's a fix."

As Max and his band-mates sat in front of Walsh, he told them: 'You know why you're here. Guys, I've thought long and hard. It's been a really difficult decision. It's one of the hardest decisions I've ever had to make. Guys, you broke the rules and you stopped somebody else getting in the competition. The decision has been made: guys, you're disqualified from the competition. You lied to me.'

Max tried his best to take the crushing news on the chin. His mind might have ventured back to when he was told that his football injury had ruled out a career in the sport. Now here he was again, on the brink of the live shows of *The X Factor* only to have his dream taken from him once more. 'We broke the rules,' he admitted. 'It's not *The X Factor*'s fault, man.' Seeing the heartbreak that Max and the others were going through, Walsh was moved to the brink of tears himself. 'I'm really sorry,' he said. Slowly the band rose to leave the room, with Max moving most slowly. Struggling to contain his tears he gracefully shook Walsh's hand. Inside, though, he was in pieces.

The newspapers again covered the story in sensational style, as they do any 'scandal' to break from the ever-popular *X Factor* franchise. Cowell told *The Sun*: 'They misled us. It wouldn't have been fair to allow them to deprive another act of being in the finals.' A spokesperson for *The X Factor* confirmed: 'It is with regret we've had to eliminate them from the remainder of the competition due to this breach of the rules.' Max explained that the band had never been confident they would reach the live shows, which is the only stage in the competition where them having an existing management deal would have been an issue. 'We obviously believed in ourselves,' said Max, 'but we didn't know we were going to get that far. We got to the final twelve, and to the point where you have to sign a management contract with the show. It was then we had to say we already had a management contract.'

Fellow band member Jamie Tinkler added: 'They never asked us if we had a manager. At the first audition they gave us so many forms to fill in, and I felt we were rushed through them. I know we should have read them in detail but I didn't think we were doing anything wrong. We knew you couldn't have a record deal but we thought a management deal was OK. In the future *The X Factor* need to make it more clear. I would hate anyone to go through what we have. We're heartbroken.' Jamie added that they were taken by surprise when they arrived at the fateful confrontation with Louis Walsh. 'After the story broke in the paper we were told it could be OK if we terminated our management contract, so that's what we did. We were called down to London and thought we were going to speak to a lawyer and were all hopeful. But as soon as we walked in the room and Louis was there with a copy of the *Mirror* we knew that was it.'

In the same feature, Max was in less contrite mood when he said: 'We've been made an example of and it doesn't seem fair. We didn't cheat. A few of us broke down. Even some of the film crew were in tears, we'd all grown really close. I regret we had to lie about how we got together but I didn't think we were breaking any rules.' These sentiments were less humble and forgiving than those that he expressed at the time of Avenue's elimination from *The X Factor*. Even later still, Max added: 'I was devastated. Simon Cowell is responsible for one of the lowest points of my life ... I thought it was all over. But I don't hate him.'

However badly the band felt for themselves, the truth was that their *X Factor* journey was over. True, Max had progressed much further this time and made more of a splash. In the final analysis, though, he had once more failed in his quest. Avenue had to sit and watch as Eton Road were

– to their own disbelieving delight – reinstated in the contest. Ultimately, Eton Road finished fifth in the competition, a marker perhaps of what fate might have awaited Avenue had they remained in the contest rather than being sent home. They could therefore view their elimination as a cruel blow, which denied them considerable television exposure, or as a lucky escape from what could have been a mediocre showing in the finals, leading to nothing of any note for Avenue.

'I think it's worked out for the best, looking back on it,' said Jonny. 'At the time, I was devastated, we all were. We'd told our families, we'd filmed the reveal, we'd met all the other final twelve and everything.' He then explained what the next step was. 'Now, though, we have a record label and a management company that let us have lots of input in what we do, like we chose the photos for the artwork on our single and things like that.' Max, too, had no hard feelings looking back at his *X Factor* encounter. 'I loved it! I thought it was great.

twittertwittertwittertwittertwittertwittertwittertwittertwittertwittertwittertwitter

JayTheWanted What's a glabella?

9:46 PM Sep 15th via web

I don't think it is a bad avenue to go down. Look at JLS – It didn't do them any harm!' He added that the disappointment merely spurred him on to succeed. 'We got thrown out and disqualified, so it definitely made me more hungry for it,' he said. 'I've learned since then and it's made me stronger.'

"It wasn't like we did it for the exposure."

THE WANTED

Max and the other members of Avenue had to pick themselves up, dust themselves down and carry on as best they could. Looking back on the furore, Max was ultimately placid about the whole thing. He said: 'It wasn't like we did it for the exposure. We genuinely believed we were in the competition like everyone else, but because we had a manager we got disqualified. We're not bitter about that because at the end of the day rules are rules and we broke them.'

Moving onwards and upwards, they signed to the mighty Island Records, making them label-mates of bands like The Feeling, Mika and Sugababes. Island Records' A &

R man, Louis Bloom was confident of their chances. 'The pop press and Saturday morning pop TV might have disappeared, but fourteen-year-old girls who fall in love with boy bands are still out there. Avenue have the songs, the looks and the moves to appeal to that audience and the voices and star quality to appeal to their mums.'

They were managed by Crown Music Management, who also looked after the affairs of the aforementioned Sugababes, a pop sensation of the twenty-first century and an example for all bands to aspire to in their sheer professionalism and work ethic. Mark Hargreaves, MD of Crown Music, also felt that Avenue had a bright future as part of a fine tradition. 'Since the very origins of pop music, teenagers from every generation can recall a boy band that became their soundtrack to falling in (and out) of love as well as providing their essential weekend party tunes. The best of these boy bands stand the test of time in every fan's memory. Avenue are here to bring on the pop soundtrack for the noughties generation.'

The band moved in together and lived in London. Five lads in the same house; it must have been a lively (and quite possibly smelly) place. It was a five-bedroom Victorian house in Camden Town, north London. 'It's an absolute mess,' Ross confirmed, before pointing the finger of blame for this at Max. '[He] and Andy are like slobs, Scott's probably the tidiest, maybe me too. We're loving it, we're best friends who get on really well. We have a few niggles here and there, but nothing too serious.' Max told *Metro* that they got along well, with the beautiful game being the only source of contention between them. 'We all get on great,' he said. 'We only argue when we've had a drink and it's usually about football. I'm a City fan, being from Manchester, Andy's a Liverpool fan, Jonny's a Blackburn fan, Ross is an Aberdeen fan and Scott's an Ipswich fan.' There was always plenty to argue and banter about of a Saturday afternoon in the Avenue household, then!

The band kept a blog on its MySpace profile, which offered a fascinating insight into the lifestyles and habits of each band member, including Max. One September day he updated the blog to 'fess up to some wild partying the previous evening. 'I'm

Above: New kids on the block: the boys pose backstage at the Capital FM Summertime Ball at Wembley Stadium in June 2010.

Below: Working the crowd on the Capital FM stage.

Above: Mucking about before the O2 Arena gig to celebrate the Transformation Trust's first birthday, July 2010. Did someone step on your toes, Max?

Below: Fans queued for hours to get a glimpse of the boys at Epsom Racecourse in July 2010.

Above: An acoustic session for Capital FM, later that month.

Below: Signing copies of 'All Time Low' at Nottingham HMV.

Above: Performing at G-A-Y club in London on 31 July 2010.

Below: Tom opens the champagne early – 'All Time Low' is announced the official number one single the next day.

Left: Posing for the camera before performing on the German music show *The Dome* in August 2010.

Below: They received a rapturous response from the German crowd.

Right: A heavenly trio ... Nathan, Max and Tom work the crowd during the filming of the finale of Disney Channel's TV talent show *My Camp Rock 2: The Final Jam* at KOKO in London.

Above: The boys perform in aid of Help for Heroes at Twickenham Stadium in September 2010.

Below: Looking fresh-faced before the concert.

Above: The band perform at the Brit Awards 2011 Nominations Announcement, where 'All Time Low' was put forward for British Single.

Below: Not short of famous friends, the boys help Justin Bieber switch on the Westfield Christmas lights, November 2011.

Above: Celebrating in style with the Saturdays at the Perez Hilton One Night in LA event in September 2012.

Below: The band are clearly loving every moment as they pose with fans at Macy's Thanksgiving Day Parade in New York.

actually feeling a bit rough today,' he admitted. 'We went to an ITV party last night, then Scott went to a party for *OK!* mag and the rest of us went to the Embassy club 'til about 3. Saw Simon Webbe there. I tried to do a bit of dancing but couldn't really pull it off, I'm more of a hanging-by-the-bar kind of guy. I didn't get up until very late, my head feels like a cabbage! My normal hangover cure is just to go for some food and get a paper, so I might do that now.'

THE WANTED

Some of the band's material was written in conjunction with Anders SG, a member of the pop band Alphabeat, and other songs with the highly successful hit-writing machine known as All Around The World. Max's band-mate Ross described their music as, 'Poppy in that they're catchy, but they're the kind of tracks that you could listen to in clubs as a dance tune, or in a bar. Pop has changed – it's not about cheese anymore. You can make pop music that's credible.' Scott added: 'It's about having good tunes with meaning. And if a tune's good, everyone will like it.' Max was a little more concise when describing their sound … he called it 'mint'.

In the summer of 2008, Avenue went on a tour of British schools, to whip up interest in their music. As Max told the website DigitalSpy, it was not only the girls who enjoyed the performances. 'The boys love it too,' he said. 'They thought we'd come out and be like a lot of boy bands they've seen, just dancers who mime, but we were completely not that. They really liked our songs and a lot of the kids liked that we weren't doing choreographed moves.' He also remembered that '80 per cent' of the schoolchildren they performed in front of remembered *The X Factor* controversy of two years previously.

A more memorable moment of the school tour came during one performance when two girls fainted and another wet herself. 'They were jumping up and down screaming then they started shaking and then fainted,' recalled Max. 'The other girl was sitting in the front row and when she left there was a puddle on her seat.' He looked on the bright side of the episode: 'I think she was about thirteen or fourteen – she just got so excited. I guess that's the ultimate compliment!' Still, it was a very visual introduction for Max to the excitement that boy bands can provoke in their audiences.

Since joining The Wanted Max has become more accustomed to this sort of excitement. But as he sang to these audiences full of schoolgirls for the first time, he began to see just what effect the members of male pop bands had in front of such crowds. He liked what he saw, though there were scary moments too. In one such episode, while the band was having a fun day out at Thorpe Park theme park, a fan ripped Max's underwear. 'That was *interesting*, yeah,' recalled Max sardonically.

He was single at the time, as he told *OK!* magazine. 'I'm single, and that's cool right now,' he said. 'If the right person comes along, you never know.' Asked which 'girly habit' he would most like to see the back of, Max's reply was fulsome. 'I'd say .. . a couple of things,' he started. 'A girl that refuses to do your washing or bring you breakfast in bed,' he began, to the amusement of the other Avenue members. 'At the end of the day, right, we're the alphas, aren't we? We're the males. Traditionally, that's how the world worked – and I'm one for tradition. So, I expect my food to be made and my washing to be done. But I'm a very loving person away from my food and my washing!' Presumably his tongue was, at least to some extent, in his cheek as he said this.

At last, he was doing what he had dreamed of for so long: using his musical talent to make people happy. He was even more excited at the prospect of recording music and standing a chance of having hit records. Avenue's first single was released in the autumn of 2008. It was called 'Last Goodbye'. The promotional video was shot in a 'behind the scenes' style. Max looked fantastic, wearing a grey blazer, white T-shirt and black trousers. His hair was cropped short and he had a light, sculpted beard. Max explained why there was no dancing in the video. 'I mean, we *could* dance, but it would be dreadful,' he said. 'We're more about energy and choreography.'

Jonny Lloyd spoke of the excitement that he, Max, and the rest of the band felt at this stage. 'It's unbelievable,' said Jonny. 'Like a dream come true. It's everything I ever wanted. Most of our songs are really upbeat, but we're not claiming to be on a one-band mission to bring pop back to the charts.'

The song itself was a bright, up-tempo pop song that they all hoped would be a big hit. DigitalSpy, who said that Avenue 'have a lot going for them on paper', were also impressed with the song. 'If Westlife came out with a track like this once in a while, they'd be a whole lot more tolerable,' said the website's music reviewer, Nick Levine. The hype around the band was swelling.

The '3am Girls' from the *Mirror* newspaper are no soft touches when it comes to assessing new talent. They have seen countless acts come and go with barely a whimper, and have therefore developed a healthily sceptical eye when it comes to sifting through the hundreds of new artists who are brought to their attention on a weekly basis. Yet when it came to Avenue, the girls were cautiously hopeful. Their first story on Avenue was headlined, 'ARE CHEESY BOY BAND AVENUE THE NEW TAKE THAT?' This was an attention-grabbing headline, to say the least. The story was exciting and excited

twittertwittertwittertwittertwittertwittertwittertwittertwittertwittertwittertwitter

MaxTheWanted The sound of piano is lovely … although I may have to throw it out the window when the footy results are on! Haha

1:48 PM Aug 21st via ÜberTwitter

too. 'Are new boy band Avenue the saviours of pop?' it began. 'The cheesy boy band are already being compared to the likes of Take That, Five and Westlife. The boys Max, Jonny, Andy, Scott and Ross performed a string of tracks in front of a capacity audience in central London.'

It was an exciting story for Max to wake up to, and his family and friends were very proud when they saw their Max not just mentioned in one of the country's biggest newspapers, but being compared to one of the biggest and most successful bands in British pop history.

When he had first auditioned for *The X Factor*, Max was compared by Simon Cowell to Robbie Williams. Now, just a few years on, his band was being compared to Robbie's band Take That. Max has always been comfortable with the Robbie Williams comparisons. Indeed, as he told *OK!* magazine, he takes it as a huge boost. 'I'm the [Avenue member] like Robbie Williams, because people say I'm a bit harder,' he said. 'If I'm compared to him, I take it as a massive compliment.' He is not shy to make flattering comparisons himself. When Max was asked who would play him in a film of his life he replied: 'Based on looks and talent, I think I'd have to say Colin Farrell.'

Could Avenue's debut single possibly live up to some of the advance billing it was receiving? The answer, much to the disappointment of everyone involved, was a resounding 'no'. Sadly, it got no higher than number fifty in the charts. With this disappointing showing, the band cancelled plans for a nationwide tour and took stock of their situation. It was a terribly disappointing moment for Max, who had already experienced more than his fair share of setbacks. However, it is these moments that have built him into the mature, strong character that he is today.

Back then, Avenue continued to take part in promotional stunts to keep themselves in the public eye. Max was at the forefront of these ventures. He was already standing out as the brightest star in the band. For instance, in September 2008 he stripped for a charity venture arranged by *AXM* magazine. The pictures of Max and other male celebrities – including Swedish star Jonas 'Basshunter' Altberg, *Big Brother* star Luke Marsden and Gladiator Tornado – were published to raise awareness for Cancer Research.

In one of the racy shots Max held a road sign for Fifth Avenue to cover his modesty. Using the fame he found with Avenue for a good cause is typical of Max's positive and kind personality. Max discussed his experience the following day on the band's MySpace blog. 'I did a naked shoot for *AXM* mag, yesterday, well not quite naked, but almost,' he wrote. 'I had a good laugh doing the shoot, you've just got to not take yourself too seriously.' He wrote this post in the run-up to his birthday, and he explained he had a combination of frolics and relaxation lined up to mark the occasion. 'We're going out tonight for my birthday,' Max explained. 'I'm more of a pub man than a club man so we'll just be going down my local and having a few bevvies, then come back and have a few more. I'll be having a quiet one tomorrow, which is my actual birthday. Getting two new lizards, which is very exciting – I'm just looking at my current two lizards at the moment actually, they're so great. My mum's coming round

twittertwittertwittertwittertwittertwittertwittertwittertwittertwittertwittertwitter

JayTheWanted Me & Siva watched this movie called Awake in the tour bus – watch it!! Horrible but brilliant! X

9:39 PM Sep 3rd via ÜberTwitter

to make me breakfast – hopefully breakfast in bed! I'll spend the day just chilling out, got to be fit for Regent Street on Sunday. We're really excited and can't wait to see you all – and a big thank you to everyone who's coming along to hand out flyers for us.'

THE WANTED

Soon after this Max and his band got a major boost when they were invited to perform as the support act on a national tour for British pop/rock band McFly. This saw them play in huge venues, including Wembley Arena. With the McFly fan-base so dedicated and excitable, their fans tended to arrive early for concerts, which meant that many tens of thousands of them got an in-the-flesh glimpse of Max and his band as they played their special guests slot. Sometimes the experiences were tough – this author saw Max and the band facing items hurled at them from the audience at the Brighton Centre – but they enjoyed life on the road and wanted more of it.

Following the final show of the tour, Max looked back on a crazy evening that capped a wonderful tour. 'We did our final gig of the McFly tour in Liverpool, Andy's home town, on Saturday night,' he said. 'It was amazing, as they all have been, and because it was the last one we just kind of went for it, probably more than at any of the others. It was really special, and a bit sad, being the last one. When we left we got mobbed on the way to the car, which was good! There were thousands of people grabbing us and screaming, wanting pictures and autographs.'

To stand a chance of having a tour of their own one day, and facing more of that level of excitement from the fans, Avenue would first need to have some hits in the pop charts. One of the songs they sang during the tour that went down particularly well was called 'Can You Feel It?' It was an upbeat dance track written by The Invisible Men songwriting team. The band recorded a fine studio version of it, which was scheduled for release on 15 June 2009. Max was very excited about this. He hoped their second crack at the singles chart would be more successful than the first. An album was planned to follow in the autumn. Could that elusive first hit be just around the corner?

In December 2008, he and the band showed their caring side by playing at Booth Hall Hospital in Manchester, to cheer up the sick kids. 'We had a really good time, it was nice to meet some of the kids. One of the girls made us a fridge magnet which was dead cute, and we also spoke to one girl called Riyah who's got her own website where she tells her story, it's quite moving.' Then they were driven to Bournemouth, where they performed as the support act for The Saturdays in a concert to raise funds for the charity Cash For Kids. Another concert around this time was at Preston College, the former educational stomping ground of Max's band-mate Jonny.

Max ended 2008 by revealing his New Year's resolutions for the twelve months ahead:

1. See Man City play more often.

2. Buy more lizards.

3. Change my bed sheets at least once in the whole year.

4. Watch more television.

5. Grow my hair ... ?

The consensus among the fans seemed to be that he should *not* grow his hair. Max's close-cropped style was distinctly popular.

139

THE WANTED

But what next for the band themselves? A tour had been tentatively arranged for February 2009, but this was subsequently cancelled. 'This is out of the control of the band,' read the statement that announced the disappointing change of plans. They continued to be written about in the press, but there was something not quite right, clearly. Indeed, no amount of exposure – of any kind – was enough to conceal the awkward truth: that Avenue's music was not proving to be enough of a hit commercially for the band to be considered to have a serious future. Behind the scenes, some difficult discussions were had and some tough options considered. The toughest of all was the one they eventually plumped for: they decided to call it a day.

The band announced their split in the first week of April 2009. 'We wanted to give all our fans and champions out there a massive thank you for your support,' the group said in a statement. 'Despite having a great time together as a band we have decided to go and follow our own separate career paths. Thanks again for all your love and support for

Avenue and it would be amazing to see you guys out there along the way as we make our own separate journeys too.' It was a sad day indeed for Max, who was comforted by his friends and family.

Looking back on his Avenue period with the benefit of hindsight, Max now feels that he and his fellow band members were simply not assertive enough. 'Even when we didn't want something we didn't speak up,' he said. In the same interview he showed that he has developed a humorous perspective on the Avenue experience. When the interviewer sarcastically asked about the 'Avenue glory days', Max got the joke as he laughingly echoed the words 'glory days'. So, what was Max's final word on the Avenue experience? 'It was good. I learned a lot – that's how I look at it.' He did indeed learn a lot, much of which would come in handy when he joined his next band. Indeed, he would prove to be quite the mentor for his new band-mates.

After the break-up of Avenue, Max took some time out to reflect. He wondered what would come next for him ...

▶▶▶ 7 THE BOY BAND

ome call them a boy band, some call them a lad band. They have even been dubbed a 'man band'. What is beyond doubt is that without the existence in the first place of the boy band, The Wanted would have had no musical tradition to step into. So where did this much-admired sector of the pop industry come from?

Over recent years we have taken it for granted that groups of young men will form pop bands that see them stand in a row, singing pop songs to audiences of delighted girls. However, the boy band was actually first conceived of over half a century ago. The first act most people would regard as a boy band emerged during the 1950s.

It was with the formation of The Osmonds that the boy band genre was truly launched upon the world. From the moment that the first screams rang out at an Osmonds performance, a new exciting form of entertainment had been launched. It was one that would be very popular and make a great deal of money for those who got the format right. The Osmond brothers began their career by singing barbershop-style music in their hometown in Utah. Having been discovered during a visit to the Disneyland holiday resort in the early 1960s, the six brothers then turned to pop, and found enormous popularity during their teenage years: girls absolutely loved them.

It was in the 1970s that The Osmonds really hit the big-time, with singles such as the catchy, sweet, 'Love Me For A Reason' really connecting with their audience. Donny Osmond became the most admired of the band members, and a real favourite among their excitable female fan-base. So excited did the fans become that the hysteria around the band became known as

'Osmondmania', in an echo of the 'Beatlemania' that had greeted The Beatles.

The Osmonds became more than just a band; they became a phenomenon. To this day the members continue to enjoy success both as solo and group performers. Back in the 1970s, they quickly caused such a stir that other acts were ready to follow their example.

The next act in this procession was also a family affair – The Jackson Five. Launched in 1964, the Jackson brothers were a hugely successful act, singing sweet, poppy soul songs. In common with The Osmonds, they too had a key, central member – Michael Jackson. By the time they released their single 'I Want You Back' in 1969, the brothers were already causing excitement and hysteria wherever they went. Like The Osmonds, they also enjoyed television tie-in series, which made them all the more popular.

twittertwittertwittertwittertwittertwittertwittertwittertwittertwittertwittertwitter

SivaTheWanted Watching Batman Begins. What a cool movie!

10:15 PM Aug 11th via Twitterrific

The other 'boy band' of the times was The Monkees. In their case they were launched by a television series of the same name. The Monkees enjoyed huge popularity in the 1960s and beyond, with songs such as 'I'm A Believer' and 'Daydream Believer', which have continued to be pop anthems for successive generations.

Between them, The Osmonds, The Monkees and The Jacksons continued – in various formations – to excel for several decades. However, during the 1970s and 1980s some other bands came to prominence in this musical field. For instance, an American band called New Edition enjoyed a great deal of fame, and ultimately launched the solo career of Bobby Brown. More famous were New Kids On The Block, who were launched by the same management team as New Edition. Their first album was released in 1986, but enjoyed limited success. However, they were not about to give up that easily. The band's management convinced the record label to give them another chance and their second album, *Hangin' Tough*, was released in the spring of 1988. It made the New Kids On The Block an international sensation. They enchanted and excited the young females of the world and released further successful, smash-hit records.

THE WANTED

By the early 1990s, when most members of The Wanted were just being born, New Kids On The Block had become so successful that they were responsible for a surge of interest in the boy band. The fact that the band had a less clean-cut image than, say, The Osmonds seemed to add to their appeal among many fans. Boyz II Men were quickly launched, which further fuelled the trend. The 1990s was to become the most boy band-dominated decade in music history. The female – and some male! – music fans of the world loved them all the more, and so did the record companies.

The UK band who were to be the biggest beneficiaries of this trend were, without doubt, Take That. Initially formed as a three-piece band called Cutest Rush, they were then approached by an ambitious pop manager who was hoping to launch a British version of New Kids On The Block. They agreed to re-launch as a five-piece and chose the name Take That. Their first singles were not major hits, but the band kept working hard – including in gay nightclubs where they could market themselves to a new audience – and were handsomely rewarded. They sold 25 million records in a glorious five-year reign that included such hits as 'Back For Good' and 'Never Forget'.

As the members of The Wanted were taking their first steps in the world, Take That were dominating the pop charts, winning scores of prestigious pop awards, and enjoying sell-out tours in arenas and stadiums around the country. The lot of the boy band had scarcely been higher. By the time they split in 1996 Take That were so popular that phone-lines had to be set up to provide distraught fans with counselling and support. When they re-formed nine years later the band continued to be a huge success story, and have since taken their total of records sold to over 40 million copies thanks to the success of new anthemic pop classics 'Patience' and 'Rule The World'.

Tom was blown away by the success of the re-formed Take That. 'I love the fact that Take That have come back,' he said. 'I was so surprised when "Patience" came out. I've got massive respect for Gary Barlow in particular. To reinvent a new sound for them was incredible.' The Wanted enjoyed a bit of banter between themselves when asked by 4music.com which member of Take That each of them most resembles.

Jay: 'We've actually talked about this before amongst ourselves. I'm Howard, because he dances.'

Tom: 'Who was I?'

Jay: 'Mark Owen.'

Jay: 'And Siva, you were Jason because he was a model.'

Nathan: 'And I was Gary, because I play the piano.'

Max: 'That leaves me with Robbie. I'm just gonna go and chill with Guy Chambers.'

THE WANTED

While Take That were enjoying all this success, there were other groups who proved that the boy band could be a hugely profitable machine. In 1996, *NSYNC were formed in Boston. Over the next four years they topped the charts across the world, with their leading member, Justin Timberlake, becoming a hugely successful solo star and an enduring pin-up. They were also marketed cleverly, and a range of spin-off merchandise sold so well that music was only one of many massive income revenues that the band produced. Their image was a touch more 'rough and ready' than some other boy bands, showing that to be successful in that market the band members would not necessarily have to be seen as angelic innocents.

"I love the fact that Take That have come back."

A UK band that also adopted a rough-and-ready image in the early 1990s was East 17, and it's this sort of look that bands such as The Wanted have taken keen notice of. Indeed, as Max said, they are aware that some people see them as more of a 'lad band' than a 'boy band'. He is happy with a number of different tags. 'We're not bothered what you call us,' he said. 'We're just average lads, from working-class backgrounds. I'm from Salford, for example, and Tom's from Bolton. We haven't changed the way we live. As long as we don't get called "man band" just yet – that sounds a bit strange!' Too late, Max. That description has been used for you in several quarters.

Another American boy band who followed the path of a more 'street' image (and therefore influenced The Wanted further down the line) was the Backstreet Boys. Formed in Florida in 1993 they had a run of enormous successes between 1997 and 2001. They have sold over 130 million records and all of their seven albums went to the top ten of the American pop charts. When the Backstreet Boys re-formed in 2005 they found further success. Their image is in certain ways close to that of The Wanted. They are cute and appeal to girls, but they are no soppy pop puppies. Like The Wanted, they had a 'baby' figure in the band (youngest

twittertwittertwittertwittertwittertwittertwittertwittertwittertwittertwittertwitter

MaxTheWanted Mornin all! Just woke up to the sound of Tom snoring and rattling room-service dishes ... I think I might have to get involved!

10:48 AM Aug 22nd via ÜberTwitter

member Nick Carter) who in their case was hired at the tender age of twelve, even younger than Nathan Sykes was when he joined The Wanted at age fifteen.

But there's another, smaller country that has produced its fair share of massively successful boy bands: Ireland. Boyzone were first formed in 1993 by Irish pop manager (and future *X Factor* judge) Louis Walsh. Their first single was a cover of the classic soul song 'Working My Way Back To You', and it reached number three in the Irish charts, and their debut album *Said and Done* made it to the number one slot in the UK and Ireland. In total, six Boyzone singles hit the top of the charts in the UK, and four of their albums did just the same. In total Boyzone have sold around 40 million albums – an amazing figure for an Irish band. But Louis Walsh was about to launch an even more successful boy band from Ireland.

Westlife was launched by Walsh in 1998, with the assistance of Boyzone member Ronan Keating, who took on the role of mentor. At this point, Simon Cowell was with BMG Records, and signed them to his label. The rest is history. Westlife's first seven singles all went to number one in the UK charts and they have had fourteen number one hits at the time of writing, including 'Flying Without Wings'. Only Elvis Presley, the Beatles, and Cliff Richard have hit the top spot in Britain more often. Worldwide, they have sold nearly 45 million records.

Their image is quite different to that of The Wanted. Westlife have become recognized as a band of well-behaved, innocent boys who sing easy-listening tunes. While The Wanted respect the success that Westlife have enjoyed, they are keen to carve out a different direction and image, one closer to another band that Cowell also signed around the same time.

After auditioning in response to an advertisement placed in *The Stage*, Five were put together in 1997 by the team behind the Spice Girls. Cowell signed them to his label and by the time they split up in 2001 – saying they could 'no longer do justice' to their fans – they had sold almost 20 million records and enjoyed eleven top ten singles and four top ten albums in the UK. Their music was flavoured with a hip-hop vibe – and they were not scared to admit that they liked to party. Band member Ritchie Neville's colourful love life with actress Billie Piper was just one of the many tabloid stories they generated. In this sense they updated the boy band genre in the UK, even more than East 17 had.

In the twenty-first century the boy band has further mutated, with bands like Busted, McFly and the Jonas Brothers bringing the guitar into (or back into) the field. They have shown that boy bands can rock as well as pop. With several Wanted members proficient players of the guitar, this development is one they fit into to an extent. While acts like Westlife continue to enjoy success with their more traditional boy band image and sound, the genre has been re-invigorated by the guitar bands, leaving some to wonder whether the more traditional format (four or five young men performing in a line without instruments) was over for good.

Then, another boy band entered *The X Factor* in 2008. They finished runners-up but became – in the eyes of many – the true winners. Their name was JLS and their amazing success story gave boy bands a new lease of life.

Forming their name from an acronym of 'Jack The Lad Swing', JLS are a four-piece vocal group who signed to the Epic

Records label (part of Sony) shortly after finishing second to Alexandra Burke in the 2008 competition. Their self-titled debut album went straight to number one in the UK chart, selling over 1 million copies. Their first two singles also hit number one. They have also enjoyed a sell-out tour and won numerous music awards, including two BRITs. They have also signed a deal with an American label, who have high hopes for their prospects in the States. Their lives have become the subjects of tabloid newspaper fascination. No wonder they are so often spoken of as, effectively, the 'real' winners of *The X Factor* 2008. If he had not found a place in The Wanted, Max might have watched the success of JLS with a heavy heart, wondering what could have been for Avenue had they not been ejected from the previous year's contest.

Instead, Max has had the pleasure of making it big himself with The Wanted. While Max and his band-mates have often been compared to JLS, they are their own entity, with an image and career path of their own. Although two of their number had previous, separate experience of *The X Factor*, the formation of The Wanted had nothing to do with that talent show. Despite that, their rise to fame was just as speedy – if not more so – than graduates of reality television have enjoyed. The Wanted came together, as Five did, as a result of auditions advertised in *The Stage*. With JLS reigning supreme, Take That (currently including Robbie Williams) provoking huge excitement in their second incarnation, and Westlife emerging refreshed from their rest, the boy band would appear to be ready to dominate the charts and arenas again. Over half a century after its inception, the boy band is back.

As we have seen, throughout its history some of its number have tried to distance themselves from that tag. Not The Wanted, though. As Max told the website Popjustice: 'We are a boy band. We're not going to try and hide from that.'

Indeed, when 4music.com asked them how they felt about the label, they could scarcely have been more comfortable with the moniker:

Jay: 'It's an ace thing. We want to bring boy bands back.'

Max: 'If we were called something else, I'd be a bit worried.'

Tom: 'Girl band?'

Max: 'It's fine being called a boy band because that's what we are, even though it's an illegal word nowadays.'

Asked why they thought the term had assumed negative connotations in some people's eyes, Max replied: 'I think it just got to the point where boy bands were totally uncool. If you even admitted to half-liking one, then you became un-cool.' Tom explained why he felt this had changed in recent times. 'JLS has brought it back massively though. That paves the way for us to make boy bands cool again.'

Perhaps, ultimately, The Wanted cannot be compared to any other band. Jay certainly thinks so. 'I was a total geek when I got in this group and decided to thoroughly research boy bands,' he told *Metro*. 'I haven't seen one we're similar to. Westlife just stand there and sing; we jump around like idiots. We have dance routines but we're not as good as *NSYNC. I think we're a new species band. Although I might be flattering myself.'

The auditions would change the lives of the five members forever …

twittertwittertwittertwittertwittertwittertwittertwittertwittertwittertwittertwitter

TomTheWanted Topman has disappointed me today.

1:40 PM Aug 3rd via ÜberTwitter

▶▶ 8 TOO COOL FOR SCHOOLS

n 2009, Maximum Artist Management – who already looked after The Saturdays, one of the biggest girl bands of the moment – placed an advertisement in *The Stage* magazine. It was to prove a wise move. The audition process went on for nine months – and at the end of those nine months there was not a baby to be shown for it, but instead a wonderful boy band called The Wanted. As Jay explained: 'The woman who put The Saturdays together held a massive audition and we all went and got put together.' He personally had nearly given up on ever succeeding at an audition. 'I failed at every one until this, which is lucky. I was going to dance auditions but I was too skinny and geeky. So I went for more alternative ones, for this and a circus audition. I think this is a bit better than joining the circus.'

Nathan, Jay and Tom were the first to be auditioned. Each appeared nervously, did their thing and hoped it would be enough to win a recall. It was only later that Siva and Max joined the process. As Max recalled, 'It took like nine months, but they eventually ended up with us five guys.' The fact that The Wanted have been so open about how they were formed is significant. There is, after all, no reason to be in the least ashamed about being in a band formed via the audition process. However, with musical snobbery being what it is, such honesty is rare. 'We're manufactured but we're not gonna try and get away from that fact,' said Tom.

The audition process is cruel, though. So many young men queued up to take part in the auditions, and all but five walked away disappointed. As Siva explained, he was not the only family member to audition for a place in the group. 'I got spotted on the books at a model agency and was asked to audition,' he said. 'My twin and my elder brother also auditioned, but it was only me who got in. My twin is happy for me, but my elder brother is still gutted.'

Finally, at the end of the process, the management had their five boys. 'It just happened,' said Jay. 'It all came together – and I don't know how.'

Tom believed that it was their differences – in personalities, ages, heights and interests – that made them click. 'We're all really different characters and we all get on so well,' he said. All the same, he was rather surprised by his interest in the band. 'I always wanted to be in music but didn't really know how, this was my first ever audition, if you asked back home I'd be the last person people would say would be in a boy band, but The Wanted's just the sort of boy band I'd be in!'

The band were taken on a series of activities and away days and evenings out, to help them get to know each other. The management were in no mood to hang around – they wished to launch The Wanted quickly. So they were keen to get the boys to form a bond as soon as possible. It could have been difficult, but with this mix of personalities, the bond formed reasonably fast. As Max said: 'It's one of those things where you try and make more jokes than you normally would. "I'll just try and be funny …" I'm sweating now at the thought of it. But we got on pretty quick, to be fair.'

There was banter from the off. Well, with a group of young men thrown together some brutal humour was bound to be part of the equation. As Jay quipped: 'As soon as Siva came in, I wanted to leave.' Max joined in, saying: 'I thought his identical twin brother was better looking.' However, these were just jokes, and Siva knew it. He said: 'I think if there were too similar personalities, it just wouldn't work as we'd compete.' Tom added: 'There's something for everyone.' As Max concluded: 'We're like a buffet.'

A buffet on which the public would be keen to feast the moment it was first publicly dished up in April 2010.

First, though, there was more bonding to be done. The five boys moved into a house together in Wandsworth, south London. A BBC journalist who visited the house described it as 'shabby chic'. One of the first things on their shopping list was a table football set. This was then followed by other laddish paraphernalia. 'Got a dartboard on the door, fridge full of beer, freezer full of pizzas. What more do you need?' explained Tom. He was the member who ventured most into the kitchen. 'We have people who do it, but normally, food-wise Tom makes food for us all,' said Max. 'We're like kids and he makes it all.' Even their laundry and cleaning was taken care of by others. Max said he did occasionally feel a little uncomfortable having a stranger wash his underwear for him. 'To be fair, it's fine,' he began. 'I don't care as long as they're clean. It's harsh but if I don't see it, I don't have to worry about it. Not until she says something and then I'll be "oh God".' When asked whose bed-sheets smelt the worst, Max pointed the finger firmly at Jay. 'His lizard crawls over it all day,' he explained.

"Tom makes food for us all."

As for Siva, he quickly fell in love with their shared home in which his bed had golden sheets. 'It's great, it's like being at college – except without the scamping for money, and making a tin of beans last all week.'

Max revealed that his is the most popular bedroom in the property – for his band-mates, he meant. 'It is a bit of a lads' flat,' he said. 'No girls allowed! Everyone hangs around in my room because I'm the only one with Sky TV. Siva's got a telly too, but you slip off the silk bed sheets. And he's got candles too! He's the zen one of the group!'

THE WANTED

With them safely and happily ensconced in their new property, it was time for The Wanted to start performing live. To build up a following, the band decided to tour Britain's schools. At each establishment they would play a short set, but a set long enough to work the fans into a frenzy of excitement. In this reality-television age, this might have seemed a strange way to launch a band. After all, each gig would only see them playing in front of a hundred audience members at most – hardly mass exposure. But this is a tried and tested method that had reaped rewards for other bands in the past. 'It's quite an old-fashioned way of doing it, like Take That and Peter Andre did all those years ago,' as Nathan told the *Reading Chronicle*.

The night before their first school gig, Siva admitted to having 'butterflies in my stomach'. The following morning he said he was 'stunned' with nerves and excitement. 'Just don't puke on my sheets,' said Jay, whose bed Siva was sprawled out on at the time. Max, meanwhile, said he felt 'awful' and had a bad throat. He tucked into porridge with honey to try and ease the discomfort. However, by the time they hit the tour bus they all felt much better, and the banter and jokes echoed round the vehicle. Their first concert was at Croydon's Addington High School in March 2010.

On arrival at the school they used the headmaster's office to relax and prepare themselves in. They supped their way through numerous cups of tea. More jokes were

twittertwittertwittertwittertwittertwittertwittertwittertwittertwittertwittertwitter

MaxTheWanted OK, I hold my hands up … yes … I am listening to All Time Low full blast and singing along!

4:03 PM Sep 15th via ÜberTwitter

swapped, as the boys struggled to contain their excitement. Then it was time to move to the stage to perform the soundcheck, during which they not only tested the sound levels, but also performed their moves for each song. When it came to time for the performance proper, they took to the stage to the sounds of *The Magnificent Seven* theme tune. The Wanted were the magnificent five!

They performed four songs, including 'All Time Low' and 'Heart Vacancy', on a simple school stage. It was a small and humble platform but the boys still danced and strutted around it as best they could. For The Wanted any performance is to be treated like a huge one, wherever it takes place. The gig was recorded on video-phones by girls in the audience, who might have sensed that they were seeing the first performance by a band who would go on to make it big.

Although their performance was not as slick as some of their later ones, The Wanted can look back on that footage with pride. Compared with the hellishly embarrassing footage of the first performance of Boyzone (who infamously danced ridiculously in front of a bemused studio audience on Irish TV programme *The Late, Late Show*) this was slickness itself. While onstage, they made sure they plugged their Facebook and other online presences to the audience. The Wanted are ever the canny operators.

Backstage, after their performance, they recorded a video message to the pupils of the school, which would be uploaded onto their increasingly popular YouTube channel. 'We're The Wanted,' said Jay at the start of the message. They thanked the school for having them and asked for feedback to be sent in via their Facebook account. 'Let us know which was your favourite song,' said Tom. Max chimed in with, '"All Time Low" is awesome. It's our first single. So if you go for that, then it makes us feel better. So if you voted for the other ones then we'd have failed.' However, he said it with a cheeky glint in his eyes. As Max and his fellow band-mates knew, they had succeeded in style. The girls at that and subsequent school performances loved them. During 'All Time Low' the kids were off their feet and jumping along to the catchy tune. Talk about a thumbs-up!

They continued to tour schools, and each time they recorded personalized video messages for each of the schools, which included the Bristol Metropolitan School, the Alderman Blaxill School in Winchester, the St Gregory's Catholic Middle School in Bedford and the North School in Ashford.

There were many, many more stops on their tour of Britain's educational establishments. In an interview with the website DigitalSpy, Nathan expanded on why he so enjoyed the school-touring process. 'You get to meet all the people who like your music. The last time we did it, when we got to the last song that they'd been hearing on the radio, they just stormed the stage. We were like, "Oh my God, we're really scared"'. It was the first outbreak of Wanted-mania!

However, as Jay admitted, the school gigs were a hard slog at the beginning, when the band were less known. 'At first they didn't care. They looked so bored as if they'd prefer to be doing maths but as things went on we got a really good reaction. Especially at girls' schools. They scream to the point where you think they're going to hurt themselves. It's invigorating but also a bit scary sometimes.' Max agreed. 'They're much more rowdy than I thought they would be,' he said. 'We took that route mainly because of how difficult it is for boy bands to break out,' added Nathan. 'There's only JLS out there and they came off the back of *The X Factor*, which is obviously the best leverage you can get right now! I guess we took the ground-up approach and decided the school gigs were the only way for us to build a strong fan-base.' That decision has proved to be a wise one, as The Wanted's fame has grown sensationally quickly.

As they had begun to build a strong fan-base, it was time for The Wanted to prepare for the release of their first single. They had been busily working with songwriters, building up a raft of possible songs for release. To this end they had moved around Europe, working with some of the world's finest pop songwriters, from Danish pop maestro Cutfather

(Christina Aguilera, Pixie Lott, Santana) in Copenhagen to Rami & Carl Falk (*NSYNC, Britney Spears) in Sweden. Back in the UK, they worked with hit-makers including Steve Mac (Kelly Clarkson) and Guy Chambers (Robbie Williams, James Blunt) to perfect their state-of-the-art modern sound. Their time with Chambers was particularly nerve-racking for the band. Chambers has won countless awards, including BRITs and Ivor Novellos, for his work with Robbie Williams on songs including 'Rock DJ', 'Feel', 'Let Me Entertain You', 'Angels' and 'Eternity', which are some of the most memorable and era-defining tunes of the members of The Wanted's lifetime. It was no wonder they felt anxious when they met him.

'Working with someone like Guy was pretty daunting at first, he's a bit of legend isn't he?' said Siva of the experience. This is an interesting signpost to where The Wanted were at this early stage of their career. While their fans were becoming more and more excited to meet them,

twittertwittertwittertwittertwittertwittertwittertwittertwittertwittertwittertwitter

JayTheWanted Was 'All Time Low' on Coronation Street or has someone been eating special brownies?

8:15 PM Sep 10th via ÜberTwitter

The Wanted were, in turn, in awe of others. Not least Chambers. 'I nearly pooed my pants,' explained Nathan helpfully. However, the band soon relaxed and enjoyed working – and partying – with Chambers. 'Guy's a bit of a legend,' said Tom. 'We were all a bit like: "It's the guy who wrote 'Angels'!" It took a couple of days for us to get to know him, but he's so down to earth, I've never met a guy like him. He's brilliant. He throws the best parties, too!'

However, it was not Chambers who wrote their lead-in single, 'All Time Low'. 'It was written by a guy called Steve Mac,' explained Tom. He then explained how the band first met Mac in a nightclub. 'He came over to us and said, "You're The Wanted boys, aren't you?"' When Tom realized who he was he felt star-struck. Jay, though, had already noticed Mac approaching. 'I saw him coming through the crowd, and I thought, 'Oh my god! He's going to talk to us!'

The song 'All Time Low' had actually been written a long time before it was chosen to be the band's first single. One of the team that wrote the song was Ed Drewett, who was just twenty-two years of age when he co-wrote it with Wayne Hector and the aforementioned Steve Mac. Drewett has since gained a great deal of kudos in the record industry because of the song. 'For me it's been a textbook development of a songwriter,' said Mike Sault, who signed Drewett up to Warner/Chappell in 2008. 'He walked through the door in early 2008 and we did the classic publishing thing of putting together some choice collaborations for him.'

There was a connection with Robbie Williams though, as 'All Time Low' was written with Robbie in mind. 'It was initially written for him but it became apparent a bit further down the line that it didn't quite fit with the rest of the album we were aiming for,' said Sault. '[The Wanted's team] heard it and they asked if they could have it. We gave it to them and the rest is history.' Sault adds that after 'All Time Low' became such a success, we should expect to hear more hit songs from Drewett in the near future. 'The fact his first proper release as a single has gone to number one, that's going to continue,' said

Sault. 'That train has left the station now. We're very much not machine-gunning it, but we'll encourage that and continue that as well.'

It was an interesting choice for their debut single, not least because of its melancholy theme. 'It is a bit depressing to be fair,' Nathan told *T4*. 'It's about when a girl is on your mind and you can't do anything, concentrate on anything.'

THE WANTED

Just as the band have differing looks and styles of vocal, so do they view their own material differently. Although they all love it, each of them sometimes picks a different thread out of it. During a chat with *4Music*, the boys held an interesting exchange of views that showed their different perceptions of the song that launched them.

Tom: 'I suppose it's got a bit of indie-pop.'

Siva: 'I wouldn't say it was indie.'

Max: 'It's under the heading of pop though. Dead-good pop.'

Nathan: 'It's anthemic.'

Max: 'When we first heard the song, we thought, "That's a good tune." Luckily enough, they allowed us to have it.'

It is indeed a good tune. It is catchy, memorable and the chants are as infectious as pop comes. A favourite and almost iconic aspect of the song is the strings that start it. The website TeenToday described it as an 'arrogant string riff' – it is certainly catchy. 'That's my favourite part,' Tom told MTV, adding that the way the song deftly builds into something bigger is also appealing. 'That song just summed us up,' said Jay. 'It sets our sound, doesn't it?' said Tom. 'It definitely sets the precedent of where our music should go.'

"That song just summed us up."

twittertwittertwittertwittertwittertwittertwittertwittertwittertwittertwittertwitter

MaxTheWanted Landed bumpy but soundly in Germany! I fancy a currywurst – supposed to be a decent scran.

9:59 AM Aug 26th via ÜberTwitter

THE WANTED

The Wanted were speeding down the list of 'firsts' and next on that list was the shooting of their first promotional video, for 'All Time Low'. On the day, it was another very early start for them, and by the time they got to the set the anticipation was huge. Tom found the experience 'nerve-racking'. He said at the start of the shoot he thought 'Oh my God, where am I?' Nathan, meanwhile, was boyishly excited by the flares they waved later in the video. Tom and Siva swapped banter between takes about which of them was the bigger diva. 'He's got the name for it,' said Tom pointing at his band-mate, 'Siva the Diva!' There was more laughter when Jay accidentally fell over during the shoot. What a red-faced moment for the lad!

The video itself was the perfect way to introduce both the song and the band itself to a wider audience. Max said, 'It looks a little like our house when the cleaner hasn't been. We didn't want to do anything too clean-cut.' Jay took note of the fact that the location for the video was a little stereotypical of the genre. 'But to be fair, we are a boy band so you have to go to a warehouse at some point,' he said.

Around this time, they were also given media training, to help them cope with the often testing ways of the press and the media. Being a famous pop star is a far from simple experience, so this sort of coaching was very important. 'Well, basically it was like, we had to sit down and they put in a radio sort of interview situation sort of thing and they'd ask us questions and we'd have to see if we could answer them sort of on the spot without sort of hesitating or saying the wrong thing,' explained Max. 'He was asking us like simple things! Questions like what's your ideal girl! And then it would be like, "er…" , but you're supposed to just answer straight away!'

Just as they were working with leading songwriters and media trainers, so too were they working with one of the pop world's best-known choreographers. 'We've also been working with Brian Friedman, *The X Factor*'s choreographer,' said Max. Friedman is indeed familiar to *X Factor* viewers, for his much-discussed backstage work with the acts. He also had a brief stint as a judge on the show, which was where Max had first encountered him. 'I'd met him on *The X Factor* but I'd never worked with him on a daily basis. He's such a nice guy but he can be strict as well – if you got anything wrong, he made you do press-ups and squats!'

Meanwhile, the live performances and appearances continued apace. The Wanted had come from nowhere as far as the public was concerned, and they were sweeping their way into the forefront of the public imagination by popping up left, right and centre. In June, they were centre stage at the Arqiva Commercial Radio awards at Westminster Bridge Park Plaza Hotel. Other performers included solo singer Katie Melua and The Wanted's 'sister band' The Saturdays. Backstage as they rehearsed, Tom joked to their manager, Jayne Collins of Maximum Artist Management, that he had 'an entourage' in the form of his extremely attractive band-mates. 'Pity about Jayne,' joked Nathan. She told him that in return for his put-down she 'would never call him Zac Efron again'! It was all good fun, the sort of verbal exchanges that keep a band happy on the road.

When it came to the time for their performance, the boys were still practising their moves in the wings just minutes before they went onstage. If they could turn on the star quality here, their chances of extensive radio play – and with it more commercial success – would rocket. They took to the stage to polite applause of seated adults, rather than the standing screams of youngsters to which they were more accustomed. Nathan and Jay high-fived at the end of their first song, 'Heart Vacancy'. Tom then introduced 'what will be our single – "All Time Low".' They belted the song out brilliantly in front of those who could make or break its radio exposure, and the excited, noisy rapture that greeted the song's conclusion showed that the band were truly in tune with their radio-folk audience.

Next up came a more high-profile engagement – at the ITV breakfast show *GMTV*. This meant a 4.00 a.m. start for the band, which Siva found particularly painful to deal with. They had recently returned from a trip to Benidorm, and any relaxation they had enjoyed there was quickly dashed by such an early start. On arrival at the studios their professionalism kicked in and they put in extra, last-minute rehearsals in their dressing room. There were then more rehearsals to be done on-set – the band were realizing there was a lot of preparation for an appearance that would be little more than three minutes long.

Backstage, Nathan complained that the stylist had 'ripped my top off', leaving him topless. 'Yes, she ripped it off to iron it,' said the band's manager, 'that's the bit you left out'.

The performance of 'All Time Low', when it finally came, was again spot-on. Presenter Lorraine Kelly was impressed. After the show was off-air she told the boys 'Do you realize that in ten years time, someone will show you this and remind you of the first time you went on *GMTV*? That was *really* good.' The fact that a seasoned observer like Kelly envisaged such a long career for the band was promising. 'Lovely to see you, you were great,' she added. Tom admitted that he had felt nervous at the start of the song. As they left, they spoke to fans who had congregated outside.

When they arrived to take part at The Clothes Show – Live, some fans outside passed them a large wooden board, on which dozens of Wanted admirers had scrawled messages to the band. 'Max = muscle man,' read one of the less X-rated ones. 'I love you in a creepy way,' read another, while one fan had simply written: 'Tom, I want your laugh.' As Max observed: 'Not if you're a girl, surely?'

As excited fans gathered round them, one called Natasha asked for a snog from Jay. He duly gave her a friendly peck. Nathan performed the same duty with a fan called Charley. No wonder there was lots of screaming going on! They then entered the arena – complete with personal security guard, another testimony to their increasing fame. Max cheekily commented that, 'If I got old, bald and really tanned,' he would look like the guard – who might not have been sure that was a compliment, however Max had intended it.

More seasoned boy bands than The Wanted will be all too familiar with the radio tour, which is a key part of promoting a single. When 'All Time Low' was on the brink of release, The Wanted undertook their first ever such tour. The Wanted are at an advantage when it comes to their relationship with the radio industry. Their management is overseen by Global, who also own the top three commercial radio brands in the UK. Global's full radio portfolio includes Heart, Galaxy, 95.8 Capital FM, LBC, Classic FM, Gold and Xfm. So The Wanted have an immediate advantage when it comes to all-important radio play.

For the radio tour, the band began by piling into a bus and heading down to Bristol. It was a journey of banter and in-jokes about everything from combine harvesters and ladybirds to President Barack Obama. The boys in the band were learning to be comfortable in each other's company for long periods in confined spaces – something that will be key to their long-term prospects. As they moved from station to station, region to region, they were often asked the same questions on-air, but the band learned to answer each one as if they were fresh to them. Some interviewers came up with original concepts, like the station that got them to play 'All Time Limbo' live on air. Though this rather visual game was a little lost on those listening.

Again, fans congregated outside the stations to greet them as they arrived. When the band were outside The Wave station in south Wales, Max commented, 'I love the Welsh, they're great people.' To which a fan answered: 'I know we are.' Max's retort was swift and witty: 'And confident people, too,' he smiled.

Then it was back in the bus and back on the road. 'I love my job,' said a happy, enthusiastic Max. Occasionally the boys were given time off from the interviews, to have a bit of fun. Like the time they took out manually powered go-karts in a park. Their noisy, boyish delight showed just how much a bit of simple fun was needed.

It was soon back to the reality of work, though. When they arrived at the MTV studios they were confronted by the most excitable fans to date. They only expected a handful to be outside but there were scores of them, screaming their love for the band and banging on the side of the tour bus as it passed them. For such a new band to create this level of chaos was unheard of. One of the girls wore a T-shirt bearing the claim: 'Tom Parker is my boyf'! Tom took it in his stride: he and the rest of his band were fast learning to cope with the female admiration.

Well, it was hardly going to be a strain for them, was it?

▶▶▶ 9 ALL TIME HIGHS

The Wanted band members are fans of many bands who came into their own in the live arena. As the band members grew up loving the music of the likes of Oasis, Queen and Coldplay, they dreamed of one day singing to audiences of thousands themselves. This was why they had so loved their live performances. They had started in school assembly halls, quickly moving up to concert halls and then large arenas. During the summer of 2010 they progressed to even bigger, open-air events. They loved every minute ...

The annual Castle Concerts take place at the beautiful Rochester Castle Gardens in Kent in July and comprise a great set of gigs over a four-day period. Among those who have played there are acts as diverse as McFly, Will Young and Status Quo. The Wanted appeared on the third night of the 2010 Castle Concerts. Later that evening there were performances by The Saturdays and also the popular *Britain's Got Talent* winners Diversity. With such great talent coming on later, it was a big challenge for a lesser-known band such as The Wanted to warm up the crowd. However, they performed brilliantly and by the time their final song of the night – 'All Time Low' – began, the audience were eating out of their hands.

A few days later the boys were performing at the Andover Carnival. From the banners and screams that greeted their triumphant arrival on the stage, it was clear they had a huge fan-base there. One fan had even brought a large inflatable hammer with them, on the pink head of which the fan had scrawled in huge lettering 'The Wanted – We Love You'.

twittertwittertwittertwittertwittertwittertwittertwittertwittertwittertwittertwitter

TomTheWanted None of us have girlfriends ... crazy stuff!

3:58 PM Aug 24th via ÜberTwitter

All the boys looked great, with Nathan, in his Union Jack T-shirt and baseball cap, the most striking-looking on the day. After the gig they were interviewed by local DJ Steve Randall and their verdict on the experience was to say, in unison, 'Amazing!'

"The Wanted - We Love You."

Also in July, they had their first taste of singing at one of Europe's most prestigious venues – the O2 Arena in London. The occasion was the first birthday celebration of the Transformation Trust, an organization that donates funds for schools to provide extracurricular fun and worthwhile experiences for their pupils. Alongside them on the bill were The Saturdays, Stacey Solomon and DJ Ironik.

Next up, the band sang at the Lincs FM Birthday Bash, at the Grimsby Auditorium. Among the bands sharing the bill were The Saturdays and Olly Murs, the *X Factor* runner-up. Then they moved further north, to perform at the Lancashire Cricket Club. As well as adding new members to their ever-swelling fan-base, the band also helped raise money for a local hospice. Their growing popularity was clear. As Max launched into the first line of 'All Time Low', half the audience seemed to be singing along, and the other half seemed to be screaming. 'All Time Low' was becoming the hit of the summer.

Having ruled the festivals of the north of England, they then moved to Scotland for their next exciting commitment, appearing in Glasgow's Buchanan Street branch of HMV for a signing session. Fans flocked there – many having travelled long distances – for a chance to meet their heart-throbs and secure a precious autograph. Having signed away for hours the band then rushed across town to the SECC venue to appear at the In Demand: Live festival. Among those sharing the bill were JLS, Alexandra Burke, Basshunter and the often-present Saturdays.

By the time they reached the Radio City Live event at the Echo Arena in Liverpool the boys were almost becoming 'old hands' on the live circuit.

Onstage they began with 'All Time Low', much to the hysterical screams of the audience. Wanted-mania had hit town. After the song the noise of the fans became even louder as the band asked the crowd to scream at the end of a '1, 2, 3' count-in. The resultant noise nearly lifted the roof off! Then Max, wearing a blue baseball cap, led them into their second song – 'Heart Vacancy', which would in due course become their second single. Liverpool loved it.

The capital city was just as keen on The Wanted as the rest of Britain. At the Summertime Ball at Wembley Stadium in June their status as the hottest new band of 2010 was beyond denial. The Wanted had been together only a matter of months but here they were, at the most prestigious venue in London, performing in front of 75,000 people. They were in awe as they arrived at Wembley. 'We don't deserve this,' said Nathan. It was a star-studded bill to join, including Pixie Lott, Usher, Justin Bieber and Rihanna. Many bands as new to the scene as The Wanted might have folded under the pressure of performing alongside such musical royalty. However, Max and the lads were as confident as ever and looked every inch the stars they were as they sang in front of the mammoth audience. They took to the stage at 6.43 p.m. Their slot followed Ellie Goulding and preceded Tinie Tempah and the international pop sensation Justin Bieber.

What an amazing experience for The Wanted. Just months before, they had performed to audiences only dozens strong; now they were singing at one of the world's biggest venues, to a huge audience, both present at the gig and watching on television at home. At first, they struggled to suppress their awe. Nathan's grin was nearly as wide as the stadium itself, while Max triumphantly pumped his fist before a single word had been sung.

As the song progressed they were joined by acrobatic dancers, who only added to the spectacle. As the song reached its 'a-low, a-low, a-low' middle-eight chant, the band ran the length of the stage, including the walkway that protruded from it. Max seemed to go into a frenzied, trance-like state.

'Thank you,' said Max at the end of the song. 'We're The Wanted, you've been awesome.'

Backstage, the band tried to come to terms with what they had just been through. 'It was the most incredible feeling of my life,' said Tom. He added that as they left the stage at the end of their slot, the band members had compared with one another which of them was shaking most. He admitted that they had not expected the audience to be so familiar with 'All Time Low', and to sing it back to them. 'That was the weirdest thing,' agreed Jay with a proud smile.

Max seemed the most moved of all the band. He looked back afterwards at what a success the show had been and said: 'I didn't know how ... how ... how to feel when that was happening. All that was going across my mind at one point was "Don't dribble!" I was getting so excited that my mouth started watering and I thought "I'm definitely going to dribble."' The wonder and excitement in his eyes was moving to see. After all those disappointments, he had finally made it.

The band had conquered Britain and, as they pursue international fame, they have travelled round Europe. At the end of August they flew to Germany to appear on German television's biggest entertainment show, *The Dome*. As they flew out from Heathrow Airport, they were bubbling with anticipation for their trip and the chance to introduce new people to their music.

'How do you say, "Where are all the girls?"' asked Tom of their German driver as they travelled through the rain to *The Dome* studio.

Once there, they performed 'All Time Low' on a huge stage, in front of a large studio audience. *The Dome* is, in every way, a big, big show – but The Wanted looked very much at home. Both Max and Tom wore skimpy shirts, and the whole band looked sensational as they lined up to take a bow at the end of the song. Then it was time for an onstage interview, in which Tom was so keen to answer the first question he managed to bash his teeth against the interviewer's microphone. Ouch! 'That quite hurt,' he said. 'Don't sue me please!' joked the interviewer.

Then they set off on a German radio tour of cities including Munich, Frankfurt and Cologne. On arrival at one of the radio shows Nathan greeted one of the female staff with a kiss on the cheek, and was taken aback when she seemed offended by the gesture. 'She was petrified,' he said. Certainly, many of Nathan's fan-base would gleefully receive such a peck from the youngster. The next female staff member he was introduced to was a more comfortable recipient of Nathan's lips. 'Up for it,' he said jokingly, 'that's what I'm talking about!'

After an enjoyable, if very rainy, visit, they were back to Britain to appear at a major charity concert which would benefit a cause that meant a lot to all the band members – particularly Max.

twittertwittertwittertwittertwittertwittertwittertwittertwittertwittertwittertwitter

JayTheWanted Dreamed my lizard Tia got eaten, by a bigger her.

11:08 AM Sep 5th via ÜberTwitter

'A friend of mine was in the Army serving in Iraq,' said Max, explaining why he was so pleased to be taking part in the Help For Heroes concert at Twickenham Stadium. The charity Help For Heroes raises funds for wounded troops and their families. The live concert, in September 2010, was watched by 60,000 fans at the event and millions more on television at home. The band thrilled everyone with another ground-shaking performance, including a surprise use of flares, as they had in the promotional video. On the Twickenham stage they stood taller and more confidently than ever before, looking like a band who had been together for many years, not mere months.

In an interview backstage, they showed a little more of the naivety one might expect from such a 'young' band. During the chat, Jay raised a few eyebrows when he declared that the band were 'proper international stars', which though technically correct to an extent, still seemed a little prematurely confident. Max, too, slipped slightly when he spoke about their number one single and added: 'We've got another one on the way' before quickly adding that he meant another single on the way, not necessarily another number one single.

THE WANTED

The boys loved travelling round Europe and also the festival season, not least because their new lifestyle afforded them the chance to party with a little more style. 'We don't have to try to blag our way into the VIP areas any more to grab free drinks,' said Jay. 'Now we've had a bit of success and money – well, a *little* money – we can buy our own drinks. We don't have to scrounge any more like a bunch of backstage chancers.'

Not that he wanted anyone to be under any illusions that being in the band was all about fun. 'It's not quite as glamorous as you'd expect,' he added. 'We've had to work and work to get where we are. And we're under no illusion that it could all end tomorrow,' he said, showing that he had learned from his slip-up backstage at the Help For Heroes concert.

'We could still be a one hit wonder and no one will ever hear of us again. That's why we have to keep putting the hours in and hope people like what we do. We're in the car now going somewhere – not sure where. I think it's another rehearsal. Don't get me wrong. There are weeks when all we seem to do is party – and that's brilliant. But there's a lot going on behind the scenes to make it all happen. But we're having the time of our lives at the moment. So far it's living up to the dream.'

"It's a ballad, but not your typical boy band ballad."

The next part of the dream was for the band to record and release their second single, which would be called 'Heart Vacancy'. TeenToday was one of the first websites to review the song, describing it as 'a quite pretty piano ballad dressed up with a you-can-still-play-this-on-radio confident stomping beat, guitary bits and some light synthy moments at the end'.

The band felt that the song was a good contrast to their debut, 'All Time Low'. 'It's completely different to "All Time Low",' Nathan told DigitalSpy. 'It's a ballad, but not your typical boy band ballad, because there's no big "key-change-stand-up" moment in it. It's just a big, catchy record that we're all really fond of and we hope everyone else likes it as much as we do!' The promotional video, too, formed a contrast to the one for their first single, said Nathan. 'The video's less frantic than our last one. A lot of people must have looked at the "All Time Low" video and thought, "Who the hell are these guys and why are they jumping around like idiots?" This one has a storyline and we each tell a part of it. We had a lot of fun filming it.'

They flew to Croatia for the fun-packed filming of 'Heart Vacancy'. One of their first tasks was a stylist meeting, to decide what to wear for the video. As they met, the temperature shot higher and higher, prompting a few rethinks over which outfits would be best. A cooling wind blew up during the shoot but, because it was being filmed in slow motion, the effect it had on their hair complicated matters.

THE WANTED

Until now, The Wanted's very existence had been tied up with their debut song, 'All Time Low', so it was strange at first not only to be singing a new song, but also promoting it. But Siva argued that 'Heart Vacancy' is 'just as strong as' their debut. Max agreed, saying, 'All of a sudden, the beat just goes BANG!'

As well as countless interviews, The Wanted team had a much more original way of promoting 'Heart Vacancy'. They launched a competition, asking fans to name the song they would most like The Wanted to cover for the B-side of 'Heart Vacancy'. Nathan told DigitalSpy that he and the rest of the band had had a lot of fun sifting through the entries. 'We've had some hilarious suggestions from the fans,' he said. 'Some of them just want us to do their favourite song at the moment, without thinking about how we'd even begin to cover it. The suggestions have allowed us to come up with all sorts of new song arrangement ideas too, so it's been a helpful exercise.'

Nathan was asked what song from pop history he would dread attempting to cover. '"The Birdie Song",' he replied. 'Or maybe a song by the Cheeky Girls. Whatever happened to them?' The winning entry, which they did indeed cover for the B-side, was the song 'Kickstarts', originally by Example.

The video for 'Heart Vacancy' served, perhaps unintentionally, as a promotional tool for the Topman clothing brand. Max wore a pair of mustard-coloured chino trousers from Topman in the shoot – and during some other appearances during the summer of 2010 – prompting a flood of interest in the clothing item. 'The Topman mustard chino has received a phenomenal amount of attention during the summer,' said a spokesman for the popular high-street chain. 'The Topman chino is gathering a celeb following with music artists such as Max from The Wanted, and has resulted in us expanding the range for this autumn/winter, with the addition of six new colours.' Speaking to the website CELEBritain.com, Max said: 'It's all about Topman mustards! They've been like a brother to me! Through thick thin and more ... !! Take care of your mustards, and they'll take care of you!' *X Factor* runner-up Olly Murs is the latest celebrity to follow Max's lead and be seen in a pair of the now-famous strides.

The Wanted sang 'Heart Vacancy' during a 'mash-up' for an XS Session, a regular recorded feature on the *News of the World* website. The other two tracks that they included in the medley were 'Live Forever' by Oasis and 'The Man Who Can't Be Moved' by The Script. For those members who grew up idolizing Oasis, including Max and Tom, it was a special moment. Meanwhile, the bookings at home continued to flock in. They were lined up to appear at *T4*'s 'Stars of 2010' concert alongside N-Dubz, JLS, Jason Derulo, Mark Ronson and many other top acts.

The boys continue to pay tribute to the trail that JLS blazed for them. 'If they hadn't brought the whole boy band thing back,' Jay told MTV, 'I don't know if we could have actually done it,' he smiled.

'As opposed to taking them on, because we would fail, we will try and leech onto their success and get dragged up by them.' Tom added: 'We're not trying to copy them, we're trying to be ourselves. Hopefully people appreciate and like that.'

▶▶▶10 INTO TOMORROW

The Wanted have already come so far, and become famous so quickly, that it is easy to forget that not only are they normal young guys, but their connections with a more ordinary lifestyle are still intact. As they played huge concerts and enjoyed their first number one single, Nathan continued to try and juggle his band commitments with his studies. As The Wanted machine became ever bigger and more demanding, he had to make some realistic decisions. He was asked by *OK!* magazine how well it was going. 'Badly!' Nathan laughed. 'No, I did my first year A-levels and did my exams, and I've worked hard, but I don't think I'm going to continue the second-year exams just yet – I want to go back and do them properly, when I've got more time.' The way things were going for the band, that wasn't likely to be for some time yet: with a hectic schedule of live performances, TV and magazine interviews and finding 'studio time' to work on the new album, Nathan and his fellow band members were kept very busy indeed.

Still, they found time to party and, quite naturally, their wilder ways were charted by the tabloid papers, who were becoming increasingly fond of stories involving The Wanted lads. At one point during the summer *The Sun* newspaper claimed that the band went on a five-day 'drinking bender'. This included a night out at the London nightclub Aura, at which Siva was said to have been particularly 'well oiled'. *The Sun* claimed he could 'hardly string a sentence together' and the young man admitted: 'We got home at 6.00 a.m. No one remembers much.' Tom added: 'The lads were determined to get me bladdered as it was also my twenty-second birthday this week. They did – but I got a snog so I'm happy.' Max gave a sense of the price they paid for their hedonism when he said: 'It's been the most incredible week of our lives but we're all now feeling the effects of it!'

In August 2010, while most Brits were holidaying abroad, The Wanted left the live circuit and the partying behind for a while and returned to focus on recording and mixing again. 'We had a break from the studio and now we've gone back in to record a whole load of new tracks,' said Nathan. 'At the moment we've written about 40 to 50 per cent of the lyrics, which we're really proud of.'

Tom said that they had gone to great pains to create a varied album. 'We've tried to make the album so that different people can listen to it,' he said. 'Some people will like one track but then other people will like another track. It's got different genres.' Max, expanded on Tom's theme: 'We've done some more poppy ones, which I really like, and then we've done a big ballad that's got really good beats to it. We're just choosing the songs. We've got eleven "definites" and the twelfth one could be one of three.' It sounded like the album was indeed going to be a 'buffet' as the band had described themselves just a few months earlier.

Nathan spoke in detail about the work-in-progress in a chat with journalist Robert Copsey from DigitalSpy. 'We had to beg our label to give us more time in the studio because we were keen to have more input,' he said. 'To begin with, they gave us just one day to complete a track, which is difficult by anyone's standards, but it turned out that they loved what we came up with and now it's on the album. We still haven't thought of [a title]! We're going to come up with the title once the album's completely finished. Having said that, we'll probably go for something quite simple in the end, anyway.' Nathan added that there were already some stand-out tracks in his opinion. 'There's a track called "Golden" that I love to bits. It's like nothing else on the album, as it's got quite an unusual sound. For that reason it probably won't be a single, but it's a great track for the album and shows a different side to us. It takes us far away from that typical boy band sound.'

Another of the rumoured album tracks was 'Lose My Mind'. The first to hear a sneak preview of it was Olly Meakings of the website TeenToday, who was cynical about the role of The Wanted's record label in the songwriting process: 'We've been granted exclusive access to the songwriter memo for this track. It reads: "Dear songwriters, Please take the ohhh-ohhh-ooohs from Kings of Leon's 'Use Somebody' and somehow make a new song around them. Make it good will you, we masterminded top 170 chart act Mini Viva dontchaknow, Love Geffen."' Meakings was even more damning about the song 'Lose Your Mind'. He wrote that it 'appears impressive on first listen, and then fades in greatness from there'. The Wanted would learn, and learn fast, that the words of the critics are often not at all in tune with the feelings of the wider public.

It promised to be a sensational album and it was bound to receive plenty of attention; The Wanted have become tabloid and gossip magazine obsessions. Naturally, a lot of the 'red-top' newspaper column inches about the band have involved speculation over their love-lives. They have often played on the same bill as their management-mates The Saturdays, and the band make little secret of their

twittertwittertwittertwittertwittertwittertwittertwittertwittertwittertwittertwitter

MaxTheWanted Listening to MJ [Michael Jackson] in the car ... I'm actually tryin to bust out a few moves ... failing obviously!

3:33 PM Sep 15th via ÜberTwitter

admiration for the girls – in all ways. Max says The Wanted have always enjoyed their brushes with The Saturdays. 'They're lovely,' he told *OK!* magazine. 'We played football with them too. Vanessa's really good – she's wicked. Frankie's awful ... we're still talking football! They're top girls.'

The band members have been linked with a bevy of beautiful women, including some celebrity lasses. Siva, for instance, was connected in the news pages with another pop superstar – Rihanna. They were said to have first encountered one another after the Capital FM Summertime Ball in June 2010. 'It's true,' said Siva. 'I met her in a club. She is very nice and very tall. She gave me a dance. She's really nice – we did swap numbers.' His band-mates have since claimed that Rihanna and Siva ended their first evening together at the Greggs bakery, though it seems unlikely, not least because he continues to remain happily attached to his long-term girlfriend, Nareesha.

Meanwhile, Max has also been linked with an internationally famous diva. He had been thought to be single, but the *News of the World* reported he has been dating a blonde aspiring pop star called Bobbi Aney for two years. They met when trying to make it in pop, during Max's days with Avenue. Aney was in a band called Fallen Angelz at the time, alongside Mollie King, who would later join The Saturdays. Aney is now in a three-piece vocal band called Inky.

"They're lovely. We played football with them too."

But whatever the truth of his relationship with Aney, Max has also been linked with pop superstar Leona Lewis. He was seen chatting and partying with her at the Whisky Mist nightclub, when he and his band-mates were out celebrating their first number one single. Lewis herself was on one of her first big nights out following the split from her ex-boyfriend Lou Al-Chamaa, so they were both on a high.

'Leona was really letting her hair down,' an eyewitness was quoted as saying in the *Evening Standard*. 'She got chatting to Max at the bar. They all partied away until 3 a.m. and then he asked for her number. Leona's certainly not going to be short of options when she's ready to date again.' When a *Sun* reporter asked Max if he had asked Lewis out, he replied, 'That would be telling, but I went home with a big smile on my face.' However, Leona has since been reported to be dating a different man, so perhaps the rumours surrounding her and Max were a bit fanciful.

The 'sex appeal' of the band is certainly a key element of their marketing pull. They have looked to other boy bands for an example to follow in exploiting this aspect of their image. For instance, as JLS released a branded range of condoms, Tom admitted that The Wanted guys had discussed going down a similarly saucy road themselves. 'We were thinking of doing some sort of contraception pill or Viagra or something,' he said. 'We also discussed a sex toy, you know, like a cast of your own member or something. We think that would be a goer. Whose would be the most popular? Definitely not Nathan's – he's only seventeen.'

Jay added that on their Twitter accounts they received many steamy messages from their fans. 'We get sent some proper smutty filth,' he said. 'The one I can [repeat] which is no swearing is just three words. "Get in me."' Indeed, as Nathan recalled, there was once a rather X-rated moment onstage. 'I'm not sure if this counts as nice, but a fan threw a tampon on stage with "I love Max" written on it,' he said. Not that the fans were always so vulgar, he added. 'At a different gig, a fan threw her bracelet on stage – we picked it up, and all of a sudden loads of fans were chucking bracelets at us. It was both an incredibly sweet and strange experience!'

For The Wanted, as for the other pop sensation of the moment Justin Bieber, the online world has been key to raising and maintaining their profile. 'We're up against reality television shows like *The X Factor*, where people have weeks of getting to know the contestants,' said Jayne Collins, the band's manager. 'Basically, we've made our own show online and gathered fans out of nowhere. It's been very effective.'

Not that Collins is suggesting that the Internet – or any other part of marketing the band – is more important than the music itself. 'The Internet and all that other stuff is great, but if you don't have the music to back it up then you've got nothing,' she said. 'People aren't stupid.' The band members agree that their focus on the online world is a sincere, rather than cynical, ploy. 'It's all about the fans,' said Tom. 'The least we can do is speak to them. A lot of people don't take that time for the fans, whereas we take that time to speak to them.' Max added that as they spend so much time travelling it was easy for them to maintain such a high profile on social networking websites like Twitter and Facebook. 'It's easy enough, it's just like sending a text to someone. Plus, [the fans] ask some really good questions.'

The Wanted, with their fans cheering them on all the way, could afford their bullish confidence as they completed work on their debut album. With a dedicated and substantial fan-base, a number one single under their belts and a sharp management team looking after their every move, they dreamed of becoming as successful as their good friends The Saturdays – if not more so.

When asked in 2010 what their greatest aspirations were, Tom said his overwhelming desire was that they manage to crack America. Although some sniggered at Tom's daring dream of success in such a notoriously difficult market, Nathan was openly optimistic. 'Some really influential people from America have said they love 'All Time Low' and they want to hear more material,' he told journalist James Ingham. 'They're really interested, so we're going over there to see how the record label wants to go about it. But it's looking good at the moment.'

The Wanted flew to Los Angeles in September 2010, to do some preliminary promotional work.

Meanwhile they continued to adjust to their sudden fame in Britain. They were not inclined to take any of its pleasures for granted. Nathan was asked on Channel 4's *T4* what the boys would be doing for a living if they hadn't made it into The Wanted. 'We'd probably be on the dole,' he said, rather candidly. Even though they are in such a hugely popular band, they still remember where they have come from. 'It's been pretty fast, pretty mental,' said Max when asked how he had found the 'Wanted' experience so far. 'We're still trying to get our heads round it.'

There would be even more for the lads to process in the two years ahead. For they not only fulfilled their dream of success in America, they exceeded their wildest expectations.

▶▶▶ 11 THE AMERICAN DREAM

The Wanted's eponymous debut album was released in October 2010. Given the hype that had built around the band since its formation, there was an almost crushing level of expectation as the album hit the shops. *The Wanted* did not disappoint: it is forty-five minutes of marvellously mottled, refined pop brilliance. The album opens strongly with their first three singles, then moves into less familiar territory with the likes of 'Hi And Low', a gentle ballad that features brooding, almost indie-style, vocals from Jay in the verses, before the band joins him in a classic, vocal harmony group chorus. Then comes the raunchy 'Let's Get Ugly' – set to Sergio Leone's iconic musical score for the spaghetti western film *The Good, The Bad And The Ugly* – and Max's touchingly upbeat ballad

'Golden', with its falsetto vocals that surprise the listener. The album's other stand-out tracks are 'Weakness' and 'Personal Soldier', both of which were to become live favourites among the band's screaming fans.

The album was received with almost unanimous admiration from the critics, drawing comparisons to an extensive range of acts, including JLS, early-career Justin Timberlake, Coldplay, Akon, Lightning Seeds, and Wild Beasts. As such, it was an album that appealed widely; people beyond the core demographic of teenage girls could listen to it with no embarrassment whatsoever. *Heat* magazine struck the right note when it declared: 'There's something for everyone on *The Wanted* – not just for the teeny-boppers among us.'

Admiring sentiments peppered nearly all the reviews, helping to ease the album to number four in the UK charts, quite a feat for a debut work. The longer 2010 went on, the more widely the band were recognized and lauded. Later in the year they won two gongs at the 4Music Awards: Biggest Breakthrough and Hottest Boys.

So the lads embarked on their first official national tour in triumphant mood. The fifteen-date Behind Bars tour saw them play in cities across the UK, kicking off in March 2011 in Manchester, and finishing the following month in Edinburgh. The shows, some of which the author attended, provoked deafening screams and shouts from the female audiences, particularly during moments when the vocal focus was on Nathan or Max.

The band performed with such confidence and fizz that it was easy to forget this was their debut tour. The general consensus among fans and critics was that here, at last, was a boy band that not only looked good on camera and sounded good in the studio, but could also genuinely cut it live. They lacked the 'book end' members that had been identified in boy bands of yesteryear such as Boyzone and Westlife. As *MTV* thundered the morning after the first show at London's Hammersmith Apollo, 'After last night's stellar performance, it's clear to see The Wanted have truly cemented their place in the boy band hall-of-fame.'

Yet there was no time for rest or complacency. The band began work on their second album, *Battleground*, in 2011. They had trailed one of the tracks, 'Lightning', on the Behind Bars tour. Another early taster of the new work arrived in the form of 'Gold Forever', which was the Comic Relief single for 2011. But while 'Lightning' is in keeping with the edgier, rougher edges of their debut album, 'Gold Forever' is an anthem with a smoother, more mainstream feel. It cleverly welds together the ballad and the club dance floor genres, and oozes emotion. Then came a new song, 'Glad You Came', which was released in July. When the band had announced the single on Twitter they were amused by the lewd responses of many of their fans to its title.

The album itself was released in November. It peaked at number five, one position lower than their debut had managed, but ultimately it would go on to sell more copies than its predecessor.

However it was at this point that a twist entered the plot, as the band acquired more than credible rivals in the shape of One Direction, the boy band created and made famous during the 2010 series of *The X Factor*.

When The Wanted had emerged onto the pop scene, aside from JLS, there were no serious challengers to their bid to become Britain's biggest boy band. Yet just as One Direction was proving to be Simon Cowell's dream group, it was also just the sort of band to give opponents, such as The Wanted, sleepless nights. In One Direction, here was a quintet that was young, energetic, fresh-faced and determined. So The Wanted knew that they would have to work even harder to keep up and avoid falling by the wayside, as so many other pop bands have at an early stage of their career. With critics tossing around words such as 'pedestrian', 'clunky' and 'bloodless' to describe *Battleground*, the band could be forgiven the wobble in confidence they must have felt at this point.

Fortunately, they were booked into live dates supporting pop giants Justin Bieber and Britney Spears, so they had ample opportunity to exorcise their own demons live on stage, in front of tens of thousands of people each evening. As their slots were greeted with screams and applause, the band's confidence and optimism were rebuilt. They also appeared in their own right at T4 on the Beach, the V Festival and the iTunes Festival. Suddenly, One Direction did not seem such a terrifying threat.

In truth, a considered analysis of The Wanted's core fan base and that of One Direction shows that, although the bands share many fans, they appeal to subtly yet significantly different markets. Putting aside the over-hyped romantic dalliances of Harry Styles, One Direction is an essentially clean-cut band, appealing to the younger and more wholesome end of the boy band market. Members of The Wanted are, as we have seen in earlier chapters, 'rougher' around the edges, and as such, they appeal to an older, wiser – and somewhat wilder – crowd. There is room for both to thrive in the UK market and, to the surprise of many, in 2012 there would be plenty of room for both acts to thrive across the Atlantic, too.

THE WANTED

As noted in Chapter 10, for a British pop band the United States is as difficult to crack as it is cherished. One could fill the bill at a week-long festival with leading pop acts who have tried and failed there, including such musical royalty as Take That, Boyzone, Westlife, Robbie Williams, Busted, McFly and even, to a large extent, Kylie Minogue. So when The Wanted suddenly began to thrive in the US in 2012, it was a most noteworthy feat.

Just months earlier, in Britain, they had faced critical reviews of their second album and, in the face of the unstoppable surge of One Direction, articles that bordered on obituaries from some commentators. Yet here they were in America, delighting the teenage pop market and basking in the glory of it all. Following a short promotional tour of radio stations and live venues, they released 'Glad You Came' – and never looked back. The song reached number three on the *Billboard* Hot 100, selling over three million copies in the process. Although 'Chasing the Sun' did not fare as well in the main US chart, it hit the top of the US Hot Dance Club Songs, prompting raucous celebration among the band and their team.

How, people wondered, had they managed all this? There were a number of factors behind their Stateside success: a revived Anglophile atmosphere thanks to the trails blazed by Adele and One Direction; the band's edgier image making them closer to the sorts of boy bands that US fans have always liked, such as New Kids On The Block, *NSYNC and Backstreet Boys; and the wise counsel of US pop manager Scooter Braun.

Braun, who discovered, launched and masterminded the phenomenal career of Canadian heart-throb Justin Bieber, is a shrewd and highly skilful operator. There is simply no one better than him to have on your side if you want to succeed in the US pop market. He identified that the first thing he had to do with The Wanted was to slightly tweak their image so that they appealed more to American tastes.

'He bends over backwards for us,' Jay told *The Daily Record*. 'We are quite messy characters and although we are still messy, he is making us presentable to America.'

Then Braun – and Justin Bieber himself – began promoting the band on their influential Twitter accounts, prompting the mammoth Bieber fan base to investigate this young British band. This is word-of-mouth promotion on an extraordinary scale.

Noting Braun's successful promotional work, the mainstream US entertainment industry raced to catch up. The Wanted were booked to perform at the *Billboard* Awards bash. They could scarcely believe they had secured a slot at such a prestigious gathering. Jay was amazed that they were rubbing shoulders with the likes of Chris Brown and Alicia Keyes, while Nathan burst into tears after meeting the legendary Stevie Wonder.

They also appeared on landmark US television shows, including *Good Morning America*. That performance, filmed in Manhattan's Central Park, drew widespread plaudits, with influential celebrity blogger Perez Hilton writing: 'Not only did they rock Central Park, but they made sweet love to it at the same time.'

The band could hardly keep pace with the succession of Stateside folk who wanted to praise them. Even the President's wife turned out to be a fan. As Siva told *The Mirror*, the highlight of his year was meeting Michelle Obama. 'She was so normal with us,' he said of the First Lady. 'She told us that The Wanted were on her playlist. I'm sure we're on her 25 Most Played on her iPhone.'

The year 2012 was a good one for British acts in America: as of February 2012, there were five British acts in the US top 100.

THE WANTED

Meanwhile, the personal lives of the band members continues to fascinate the British public. Max announced his engagement to *Coronation Street* actress Michelle Keegan in 2011. Their engagement had a sense of haste about it, as they had only been dating for six months when they announced their plans to tie the knot. So it was not an enormous shock when, in April 2012, Max revealed that the engagement had been called off. It was a somewhat perfunctory announcement: during a radio interview in which the engagement was mentioned, he interrupted the host, saying, 'No, no, no, not anymore.'

Afterwards, he and Keegan both announced that, though the engagement was called off, they still remained an item. Soon after that, however, they went their separate ways entirely, with some bitter words exchanged between them via the media.

Tom, meanwhile, has dated the glamorous Kelsey Hardwick for over two years. Photographs of the couple on nights out show that they share a love of the wild life. In one of the ubiquitous newspaper photographs of them pouring themselves into a taxi in the early hours, Hardwick suffered a wardrobe malfunction when her frock slipped, revealing more of her breast than she might have planned. However neither she, nor Tom, were likely to lose much sleep over the unintentional indiscretion.

Nathan has been linked to a number of girls by the media, among them teenage singer Dionne Bromfield, who is the goddaughter of tragic singer Amy Winehouse. The unconfirmed reports that they are an item prompted envious anger among some Wanted fans, who bombarded Bromfield with abuse on Twitter. It was another reminder that, while pop stardom can make a young man an eligible bachelor in the eyes of millions, it can also make him a dangerous prospect as a partner. Many young women have decided the abuse and threats they receive after being linked to male heart-throbs outweighs the joys of such dalliances.

Nathan himself has said that he has received death threats after rumours circulated that he had found a girlfriend. The band has concluded that it is for the best if Nathan remains, officially speaking at least, single. As the youngest, most puppy-faced member of The Wanted, his romantic movements attract particularly strong scrutiny. 'If Nathan got a girlfriend we'd have no fan base,' Siva told *Metro*.

Siva, meanwhile, plans to marry his long-term girlfriend Nareesha McCaffrey. When asked on NBC Live: 'Do you think you're going to marry this woman?,' he replied, 'Yeah, definitely'.

For Jay, things are less settled. He has been photographed out and about with a number of 'mystery girls'. On one such occasion he stepped out with a curvaceous blonde at London's Mahiki nightclub. However, the evening ended on a sour note as he was photographed leaving alone, in tears.

"If Nathan got a girlfriend we'd have no fan base."

While their love lives continue to intrigue, the feisty feuds they spark also earn them many column inches. As their careers have progressed, the band members have become more and more outspoken. After the band met pop princess Britney Spears in Manchester, Tom observed: 'Britney's beautiful and a nice girl, but when we met her, I expected her to have more personality.' In a separate outburst, he also laid into another pop songstress, this time Christina Aguilera. 'She might not be a bitch in real life but to us she was a bitch,' he said. 'She just sat there and didn't speak to us. Wouldn't even look at us.' Even when, forty-eight hours later, he seemingly backtracked, he did so with a disapproving tone. 'We shouldn't have said it, to be honest with you,' he said. 'We just think manners cost nothing, you know what I mean?'

Yet these episodes were small fry when compared to the band's regular feuds with One Direction. When The Wanted had first emerged onto the scene, the media had attempted to hype a rivalry between them and the established boy band JLS. Now, it was The Wanted who was billed as the established act, with One Direction billed as the new boys, snapping at their heels.

Yet this time the rivalry did have a personal dimension and sharp edge. As Max told *Fabulous* magazine in November 2012: 'We're not the best of friends, so it's not like we are going to go up and start hugging and kissing. And they make little comments in interviews when we're mentioned. But they're young, and that's expected, and I laugh at it. If they're taking it seriously, then maybe that's just an age thing.' Jay was slightly more conciliatory when he added: 'I've met the boys. They're not angels, but who is?'

However, just weeks later, it seemed war had been declared. Max got involved in a Twitter battle with One Direction's Zayn Malik and Louis Tomlinson, which began when Malik called Max a 'geek'. After Max responded with humour rather than fury, Malik took another swipe, writing: 'I'm not sure why your still talking to me mate conversation ended when I called you a geek. p.s your display just shows how much of a wannabe you are :)'

Max replied: 'That's not very nice. I was just starting to like you and your RnB hits.' Tom then joined in, tweeting to Max a sour remark about Malik, who had recently had a blonde streak put into his hair. 'I think "1 stripes" got his knickers in a twist bro,' wrote Tom. If Tom had hoped to up the ante, he succeeded. Malik replied: 'Mate if I had a face like yours my hair would be the last thing I'd worry about :).' One Direction's Louis Tomlinson then wrote to Tom: 'Pipe down bad boy.'

The exchange was fast becoming the talk of Twitter, as fans of each band furiously re-tweeted their respective heroes' messages, and others merely looked on with scandalized glee at the entertaining celebrity spat unfolding on the social networking website. Further insults were traded, including Tom posting a photograph of Malik looking doe-eyed and sweet, adding the sarcastic caption: 'Bradford bad boi.'

Max then recommended that Malik, 'Stay off the bud … It clearly makes u cranky', to which Malik audaciously replied: 'Alright chlamydia boy ;).' Max chose to remind Malik that he was his junior, writing: 'shut it or I'll take your dinner money. :).'

The spat made headlines on both sides of the Atlantic. Speaking to Radio 955 in America, Max said of Malik: 'I'm not sure what his problem is to be honest. It started off that I thought we were just having a bit of banter, but he seemed to get a bit serious.' He added that he had advised Malik that if he had 'a problem' with him, then they could 'sort it out' in person next time their paths crossed. It is hard to imagine Malik relishing the chance of a physical confrontation with Max.

THE WANTED

So what does the future hold for The Wanted? Their third album, *Third Strike*, was set for release in March 2013. Nathan said that, following the rather darker mood of

Battleground, the new album would be a more upbeat affair. 'With this next album I think we're going to take the darkness from our last record but add in the feeling of our first,' he said. 'This album will be bigger and more uplifting and optimistic.'

"This album will be bigger and more uplifting and optimistic."

The earliest hints of its tone came in the form of singles 'Chasing the Sun' and 'I Found You'. The former track included the rapper Example among its composers, and featured Jay in a leading vocal role. It was released in April 2012 and actually proved to be a prescient release for the UK market as relentless rain and dark clouds ensured that Britain scarcely enjoyed a summer at all in that year. Moments of sunshine were few and far between until August, which gave a song about chasing the sun a strangely poignant relevance. (A similar coincidence had struck when Rihanna released her single *Umbrella* during another hideously wet British summer.)

The single 'I Found You' followed in November. Reminiscent of 'Glad You Came', it helped to keep anticipation for the forthcoming album on the boil. During a chat with *DigitalSpy*, Tom joked that the song's falsetto chorus was no great challenge to him. 'To be honest, the chorus is the easiest part to sing,' he said. 'Most of us could sing like that all the time if we had to.' Nathan, too, was in humorous mood. When asked, given the song's title, what was the most important thing he had lost, he replied: 'My dignity.'

More than ever, they had worked on the album with both the UK *and* US audiences very much in mind. Balancing both markets will be a challenge for the band and their team in the immediate future. The US audience is so lucrative and emotionally important to them that they dare not let their progress there slide. Yet they cannot afford to lose their popularity in Britain, either. Some of their UK fans are sensitive to any hint that the band has lost touch with them, or sold out their roots in favour of the US dollar.

But maintaining their popularity in both territories is, as the saying goes, a nice problem to have. As they prepared to release their third album, the band could reflect that many boy bands never reach a second album before imploding in the face of public indifference. Even some of the biggest boy bands in British pop history, including Take That and Westlife, would, at their respective peaks, have killed to have had a US presence to even worry about.

At the time of writing, their fan-bases on both sides of the Atlantic are as devoted to The Wanted as ever. The threat to their popularity posed by One Direction was always overestimated, and both bands have realized that their rivalry is, in marketing terms, something that benefits each of them enormously.

What, then, can stand in the way of continued success for The Wanted? The only significant obstacle could be the band members themselves. Their sensational success has come with a price to each of the boys: they have had to work incredibly hard and have sacrificed their privacy. They have shown few signs of any fatigue publicly, yet behind the scenes each member has had his moments of disenchantment. Their management, friends and family are wise to the weight of the burden fame has put upon Max, Nathan, Tom, Siva and Jay, and are supportive. As for the lads themselves, they worked so hard to get to the top, they are in no hurry to call it a day.

ACKNOWLEDGEMENTS

Thanks to Michael O'Mara, Louise Dixon, Kerry Chapple,

Chris Morris, Chris Leonard and Myma.

PICTURE CREDITS

Page 1:   John Phillips / EMPICS Entertainment / Press
Association Images (top); Suzan / EMPICS
Entertainment / Press Association Images
(bottom)

Page 2:   Suzan / EMPICS Entertainment / Press
Association Images (top); Nigel French /
EMPICS Sport / Press Association Images
(bottom)

Page 3:   John Phillips / EMPICS Entertainment / Press
Association Images (top); Rowan Miles /
EMPICS Entertainment / Press Association
Images (bottom)

Page 4:   Chris Jepson / Famous (both)

Page 5:   Florian Seefried / Getty Images (top); Sean
           Gallup / Getty Images (centre); David Parry /
           PA Wire / Press Association Images (bottom)

Page 6:   Brian Rasic / Rex Features (top); Dave J Hogan /
           Getty Images (bottom)

Page 7:   Dave Hogan / Getty Images (top); Brian Rasic /
           Rex Features (bottom)

Page 8:   Toby Canham / Getty Images for BMF Media
           (top); Charles Sykes / AP / Press Association
           Images

INDEX

Academy of Contemporary
    Music (ACM) 114
Addington High School 169
Adrienne (Max's lizard) 23
Affleck, Ben 44
Aguilera, Christina 174
Al-Chamaa, Lou 217
Alderman Blaxill School 172
All Around The World
    (songwriting team) 129
All Saints 105
All Saints' School and
    Performing Arts
    College 77–9
Alphabeat 129
Altberg, Jonas 'Basshunter'
    135, 194
Anders SG 129
Andre, Peter 169
Aney, Bobbi 216–7
Appleton, Natalie 105
Appleton, Nicole
Arqiva 181
Attenborough, David 73, 77
Attitude magazine 64
Avenue (band) 10, 27, 65,
    112–41
AXM magazine 135–6

Backstreet Boys 153–4
Bacon Theatre 98
Badly Drawn Boy 49
Barlow, Gary 151

Batman Begins 147
Beatles 48, 114, 147, 155
Beckham, David 25
Behr, Dani 93, 99
Bieber, Justin 90, 195, 219
Big Brother 135
Bloom, Louis 127
Blue 100, 114
Blunt, James 174
Bolton School 20–1, 33
Boyz II Men 87, 149
Boyzone 116, 154, 171
Bristol Metropolitan School
    172
BRIT Awards 174
Britain's Got Talent 87, 192
*Britney Spears' Karaoke
    Kriminals*
    99
Brookstein, Steve 30
Brown, Andy 114, 128, 134,
    137
Brown, Bobby 148
Bunton, Emma 104–5
Burke, Alexandra 30, 35, 157,
    194
Burnett, Yvie 117–18
Busted 105, 156

Candy, Ross 114, 128, 129
Carey, Mariah 92
Carr, Alan 27
Carter, Nick 154

Cash For Kids 139
celebrity 12, 19, 20, 22, 44, 48, 53, 63, 100, 129, 135
Chambers, Guy 151, 174–5
Cheltenham and Gloucester College of Higher Education 97
Chidzoy, Jacqueline 95, 96, 102
Children in Need 98
Clarke, Scott 114, 128, 129, 134
Clarkson, Kelly 174
Clifton, Michael 102
Coady, Nikki Dawn 102
Cobbett, Mr (teacher) 78
Coldplay 73, 191
Collins, Jayne 105, 181, 219
Collins, Phil 20
Copsey, Robert 214
Coronation Street 174
Corr, Caroline 48
Corrs 48
Cotton, Fearne 93
Council for Dance Education and Training 80
Countdown 76
Cowell, Simon 29–32, 52, 82, 112, 113–16, 122, 124, 134, 154–5
Crown Music Management 127
Cutest Rush 149
Cutfather 173
Cyrus, Miley 48

Derulo, Jason 206
Dench, Dame Judi 111
Destiny's Child 100
DigitalSpy 130, 133, 172, 202, 214

Dome, The 198–9
Donald, Howard 151
Drewett, Ed 176–7

East 17 152, 156
Efron, Zac 181
Egan, Kian 117
Elvis (dog) 32
Emma Priest Scholarship 104
Eton Road 65, 124–5
Eurovision Song Contest 66, 105–6

Fabregas, Cesc 25
Family Guy 57
Farrell, Colin 135
Faulkner, Newton 73
Feeling 126
Five (band) 134, 158
Fletcher, Tom 104
Florence 73
4Music 177
4music.com 151, 158
Friedman, Brian 180

G4 120
Galaxy 185
Gallagher, Liam 27, 47, 48
Gallagher, Noel 27, 48
George, Mark 27, 32, 34, 112
George, Max (Maximillian Alberto) 9–10, 11, 12, 15–35, 42, 51, 65, 89–90, 91, 93, 106, 111–41, 151, 157–8, 195, 196, 199, 200, 206, 213, 216–18
    acting career of 111–12
    ambitions of 24–6, 28–9, 33, 35
    Aney linked to 216–17

'big brother of the band' role of 19
birth of 17, 20
education of 20–1, 32–3
fails *The X Factor* 'boot camp' 33–5
family of 27, 32, 34, 59, 136, 141
fearless nature of 21, 31
football skills of 23–7
former band of 9, 19, 27, 65, 111–41
imposing nature of 13
injury/illness of 25–6
Leona Lewis linked to 217–18
love of lizards of 21, 23, 139
musical influences of 17, 22, 27, 29, 31–2
New Year resolutions of 139
pets of 21, 23, 32
potential professional football career of 24–6, 28, 33
retail career of 28
solo career of 20
The Wanted joined by 163–87
The X Factor auditions of 29, 30–5
tweets of 23, 27, 32, 115, 133, 153, 169, 178, 215
untidy nature of 43
see also Wanted, The
Girls Aloud 65, 114
Glades Shopping Centre 103
Gladiator Tornado 135
Glee 80, 81
Global Talent Group 120, 185

Gloucester Citizen 96, 98
Gloucestershire Echo 96
GMTV 102, 182–4
Gough, Damon (Badly Drawn Boy) 48–9
Goulding, Ellie 191
Grand Gala Showcase 98

Halliwell, Geri 65
Hamont, Ian 96
Hargreaves, Mark 127
Healy, Una 67
Heart 185
Hector, Wayne 176
Help for Heroes 200
Holder, Julie 95–6
Hollywood 111
How 2 76

i-D magazine 64
Inbetweeners, The 39
Ingham, James 221
Invisible Men 138
Ironik, DJ 193
Irvine, Eddie 63
Ivor Novello Awards 174

Jackson Five/Jacksons 67, 147, 148
Jackie and Friends Entertain 96
Jackson, Leon 30
Jackson, Michael 22, 31, 33, 63, 114, 147
Jagger, Mick 44
James, Duncan 114
JLS 29, 46, 126, 156–7, 159, 173, 194, 206, 218
John, Elton 20, 92
Jonas Brothers 156
Jones, Danny 45, 49

Jones, Rosie 48
Junior Eurovision Song
    Contest 105

Kaneswaran, Daniel 60, 63
Kaneswaran, David 60, 63,
    66–7, 68, 165
Kaneswaran, Elizabeth 'Lily'
    62–3
Kaneswaran, Gail 60, 61, 62,
    63, 67–8
Kaneswaran, Hazel 60, 61, 62,
    63, 65–6, 67–8
Kaneswaran, Kelly 60, 61, 62,
    63
Kaneswaran, Kumar 60, 63, 67,
    68–9, 165
Kaneswaran, Mr (Siva's father)
    61–2
Kaneswaran, Siva 9, 55–69,
    136, 151
    ambitious nature of 63
    birth of 57, 60
    childhood of 59–61
    confident nature of 60, 62
    family of 59, 60, 61–7
    father's death and 61–2
    follows in Hazel's footsteps
      68
    girlfriend of 69, 216
    guitar-playing skills of 59
    modelling work of 64
    musical influences of 57,
      67
    Rihanna linked to 216
    show-business aspiration
      of 59
    songwriting skills of 64
    soup thrown at 60–1
    supermodel looks of 13,
      69

The Wanted joined by
    163–87
    tweets of 61, 62, 66, 69,
      147
    twin brother of 67, 76
    see also Wanted, The
Kaneswaran, Trevor 60, 63
Kaye, Vernon 44
Keating, Ronan 154
Kelly, Lorraine 183
King, Mollie 217
Knightley, Keira 53

Lampard, Frank 25
Late, Late Show, The 171
LBC 185
Lee, Monica 21
Lennon, John 48
Levine, Nick 133
Lewis, Leona 12, 29, 217
Little, Ralf 21
Live & Kicking 93
Lloyd, Jonny 114, 125, 128,
    132, 134, 139
Longlevens Junior School 94
Lott, Pixie 174

Mac, Steve 174, 175
McFadden, Brian 67
McFly 23, 44, 49, 50, 104,
    137–8, 156, 191
McGuiness, Jay (James) 9, 12,
    53, 69, 71–83, 151,
    158–9, 200–1
    animal-loving nature of 77
    'Billy Elliot' sobriquet of
      81, 82
    birth of 73, 75
    childhood of 75
    dance auditions attended
      by 82–3

dancing skills of 78–81, 82
football doesn't interest 77,
    81, 82
education of 77–81
family of 77, 78
fun-loving nature of 76
musical influences of 73,
    83
nimble-footed nature of 81
religion and 77–8
school friends of 79
show-off nature of 76
steamy tweets to, 219
sweet nature of 13
The Wanted joined by
    163–87
tweets of 79, 80, 83, 125,
    136, 174, 199
twin brother of 76
vegetarianism of 77
see also Wanted, The
McGuiness, Tom 76
McKellen, Sir Ian 21
Marsden, Luke 135
Massive Millennium Showcase
    97
Maximum Artists'
    Management 163, 181
Meakings, Olly 214–15
Melua, Katie 181
Meteor Music Awards 66
Metro 23, 31, 76, 128, 159
Midlands Academy of Dance
    and Drama (MADD)
    79–81, 82, 82
Mika 126
Ministry of Mayhem 103
Minogue, Kylie 20
Mirror 124, 133
Misfits 73
Monkees 148

MTV 178, 186, 206
Murs, Olly 193, 206
MySpace 50, 67, 136

Nareesha (Siva's girlfriend) 69,
    216
N-Dubz 206
Neville, Ritchie 156
New Edition 146
New Kids on the Block 148
News of the World 206, 217
Notes on a Scandal (film and
    novel) 111
Now That's What I Call Music
    42
*NSYNC 152, 159, 174, 232

Oasis 27, 31, 33, 39, 48, 191,
    206
Obama, President Barack 185
OK! magazine 27, 68, 69, 129,
    131, 134, 205, 216
Olympus Theatre 96
Orange, Jason 151
Osbourne, Sharon 31, 113,
    116, 118
Osmond, Donny 146
Osmonds 146–9
O2 Arena 193
Owen, Mark 50, 151

Panel, The 66
Parker, Tom (Thomas
    Anthony) 9, 11–12,
    37–53, 75, 115, 151,
    153, 158–9, 206, 218
    accident-prone nature of
        12
    America ambitions voiced
        by 220–1
    benefit claimed by 53

birth of 39, 42
boy-next-door looks of 13, 42, 44
career options of 45–6
cheeky nature of 42, 43
childhood of 41, 45–6
distractions needed by 43
education of 45, 48, 49
family of 49, 59
football loved by 44–5, 47
guitar-playing skills of 41–2, 44, 46, 47
ideal celebrity woman of 48, 53
illness/accidents of 12, 46–7
jokes about joining JLS 46
musical influences of 39, 47, 48–9, 50
musical interest developed by 41–2
sex appeal of 44
singing abilities of 47
'snack-a-jack' sobriquet of 50
Take That tribute band joined by 50
The Wanted joined by 53, 163–87
The X Factor pre-auditions by 51–2
twenty-second birthday of 212
tweets of 46, 47, 53, 120, 159, 192
untidy nature of 43
see also Wanted, The
Penate, Jack 73, 83
Pennell, Daphne 96
Piper, Billie 156
Pirates of the Caribbean 53

Poole, Emily 96
Pop Idol 29, 103
Popjustice 158
Popstars 64
Popstars: The Rivals 65
Poynter, Dougie 23
Presley, Elvis 31, 33, 155
Preston College 139
Priest, Emma 104
Pugh, Gareth 64

Queen (band) 17, 191

Rami & Carl Falk 174
Randall, Steve 193
Reading Chronicle 169
reality TV 17, 29
Redding, Otis 31–2, 33
Ribston Hall 106
Rice, Damien 73
Richard, Cliff 155
Rihanna 195, 216
Riyah 139
Robertson, Hollie 81
Rockingham Speedway 51
Rocky 23
Rolling Stones 44
Ronson, Mark 206
Rosie & Jim 42
Royle Family 21
RTÉ 66
S Club 7 99
St Gregory's Catholic Middle School 172
Sandford, Frankie 53
Santana 174
Saturday Show, The 93
Saturdays, The 53, 67, 139, 163, 181, 192, 193, 194, 215–16, 217, 220
Sault, Mike 176–7

Schwarzenegger, Arnold 44
Smith, Megan 79
Solomon, Stacey 193
Spears, Britney 99–100, 174
Spice Girls 104, 155
Stage, The 46, 53, 102–3, 155, 158, 163
Stallone, Sylvester 23
Stars In Their Eyes 114
Status Quo 192
Steps 97
Stereophonics 47
Stevens, Cat 83
Stop the World . . . (musical) 104
Strictly Dance Fever 81
Sugababes 126
Sun, The 119, 122, 212
Switchfoot 57
Syco Music 30
Sykes, Harry 90, 97
Sykes, Jessica 95–6
Sykes, Karen 101–2
Sykes, Nathan James 9, 87–106, 151, 199, 202–3, 204, 214
    ambitious nature of 91
    bagpipe-playing skills of 106
    band commitments v. studies of 211–12
    Bieber compared to 90
    birth of 87, 91
    boyish good looks of 89
    childhood of 90
    cuteness of 13, 90, 91–2, 98–9
    dancing skills of 94–7, 101–2
    education of 94–6, 103–5
    Emma Priest Scholarship won by 103–4
    family of 90, 95–6, 97, 101
    football loved by 90
    musical influences of 87, 98–9
    People's Choice award won by 97
    piano-playing skills of 96
    songwriting skills of 105
    Sylvia Young Theatre School attended by 103–5, 106
    talent shows entered by 90, 94–104, 105
    The Wanted joined by 163–87
    tidy nature of 43
    tweets of 90, 98, 105
    wicked sense of humour of 90, 91, 93
    see also Wanted, The
Sylvia Young Theatre School 103–5, 106

T4 177, 206, 221
Tabor, Ashley 120
Take That 29, 133, 149–51, 158, 169
Take That 2 (tribute band) 50
Teenage Mutant Ninja Turtles 21
TeenToday 178, 202, 214
Tempah, Tinie 196
Thornleigh Salesian College 48
Thornton, Kate 113
Thorpe Park 131
3am Girls 133
Timberlake, Justin 152
Tinkler, Jamie 119, 123

Tot Stars 102–3
Transformation Trust 193
Trotters 44

Village People 103
Vorderman, Carol 76

Walsh, Louis 31–2, 34–5, 65,
    116–22, 154
Wanted, The:
    album of 213–15
    auditions for 53, 67, 158,
        163–87
    concerts 191–207
    debut single of 9–12, 173,
        182, 202
    fans of 12, 23, 44, 49–50,
        69, 184, 186, 192, 194
    first Number One of
        11–13
    focus on recording and
        mixing by 212
    'Formspring' Q&A forum
        of 46, 52
    heart-throb status of 13
    manager of 106
    official website of 12
    running down the street
        naked bet 13
    second single of 202–3
    sex appeal of 218
    shared home of 10
    sobriquets of 145
    tabloids chart wilder ways
        of 212
    see also individual band
        members
Ward, Shayne 35, 120

Waterman, Pete 65
Wave 186
Webbe, Simon 129
West End 104, 113
Westlife 66–7, 116, 117, 134,
    154, 155, 156
Whisky Mist 12
Williams, Robbie 31, 32, 83,
    97, 112, 134, 151, 158,
    174, 176
Willis, Matt 105
Winehouse, Amy 104
Wonder, Stevie 31, 33
World Song Contest 66

X Factor, The 17, 29–35, 103,
    116, 154, 156, 173, 180,
    193, 206, 219
    Avenue take part in 65,
        111–26
    Max and 29, 30–3, 111,
        112
    scandals 119–23, 124
    Tom pre-auditions for
        51–2
    Trevor auditions for 63–4
Xfm 185

Yazz 42
Yolanda B Cool vs D Cup 11
You're a Star 66
Young, Chris 79
Young, Sylvia 103–5
Young, Will 103, 115, 191
YouTube 51, 171

Zoo (band) 66–7

Y – B – WANTED

Newkey-Burden, Chas

The wanted.